The Spokesm

Democracy – Growing o

Edited by Ken Coate,

**Published by Spokesman for the
Bertrand Russell Peace Foundation**

Spokesman 100   **2008**

CONTENTS

Subscriptions
Institutions £35.00
Individuals £20.00 (UK)
        £25.00 (ex UK)

Back issues available on request

A CIP catalogue record for this book is available from the British Library

Published by the
Bertrand Russell Peace
Foundation Ltd.,
Russell House
Bulwell Lane
Nottingham NG6 0BT
England
Tel. 0115 9784504
email:
elfeuro@compuserve.com
www.spokesmanbooks.com
www.russfound.org

Printed by the Russell Press Ltd., Nottingham

ISSN 1367 7748   ISBN 978 0 85124 755 7

Editorial

Democracy – Growing or Dying?

This is the hundredth number of *The Spokesman*, so we are expected to have a birthday party. Nostalgia is in order at such events, and we have accordingly devoted quite a large part of this number to reproducing articles and features which involved us, with many of our readers, in a variety of campaigns to change things for the better. Sometimes these have succeeded, if only, say the sceptics, in provoking our old antagonists to find new ways to make them worse again. Sometimes they have failed, only to stiffen our resolve to try again, when times may be more propitious for their success.

There are, of course, a number of key concerns which have continuously preoccupied us. There has been no possibility of forgetting, even temporarily, the desperate urgency of the struggle for peace and disarmament. It has been quite possible, but very regrettable, to forget the struggle for the widening and deepening of democracy, and this possibility has been amply brought into evidence by the progress of sundry statesmen, not to say less elevated tribunes of the people, some of whom have opted for popular emancipation, one at a time, me first.

This kind of apostasy does discourage people, if only temporarily. If hope springs eternal, so too does the aspiration for effective power over the terms and conditions of our own lives.

Politicians commonly tell us that the major social struggles are about power. 'We need' they say, 'power to prevent the next war, or to save the environment from destruction, or to protect people from exploitation and domination.' That is one way of putting it, but there are dangers wrapped up in it. Power does not come sanitised, prepacked only for good causes. Time and again there is contrary evidence. What we really need is the annulment of power, so that none can make wars, burn the atmosphere, or lower the people into misery. Yet if we are to avoid the charge of piety, toothless anarchism, empty promises, then we have to concede that the first step to a higher freedom requires that we learn the necessary arts to stop the various evildoers who breed for us all these wars, depredations and oppressions. But if such steps are truly to lead upwards, then the higher freedom itself must always remain in mind.

Fittingly, we have chosen a number of contributions by our founder upon which to thread the thoughts of our contributors on these matters. Bertrand Russell reviewed one of our books, Max Beer's *History of British Socialism*, when it first appeared shortly after the First World War. He highlighted Beer's acute perception that the English establishment could vainly attempt to school their people in the rites of caution and conservatism, but 'in periods of general upheavals … the English are apt to throw their mental ballast overboard and take the lead in revolutionary thought and action. In such a period we are living now'. After a long and depressing lull in their energies, it could be that we may be about to see their strong renewal very soon.

Russell's appreciation of the roots of English socialism is exemplified in the article we have reproduced by John Hughes and Charles Atkinson. This was initially commissioned for a book to celebrate Russell's centenary, and was published by Spokesman in 1972.

Three other contributions which we have selected from among many celebrate the movement for industrial democracy. In one of them, Karl William Kapp draws attention to the sharp growth in pollution which has resulted from rapid industrial development. Kapp's profound scholarship recalls the natural, as well as social spoliation chronicled by Marx and Engels which accompanied extensive air and water pollution, and gave rise to an early, and profound concern by trade unions to encourage environmental protection. When we published Kapp's article in *The Spokesman*, we were able to use it as a key text for a conference on Socialism and the Environment, in which we brought together a number of specialists including F. E. Le Gros Clark and Lord Boyd Orr, and activists such as Colin Stoneman, Malcolm Caldwell and John Lambert, who agreed to continue their work by establishing the Socialist Environmental and Resources Association, which carries on to this day.

Quite different but every bit as audacious is the contribution from Mike Cooley, which starts from the same premises, but, based on the author's profound experience of trade unionism in a high-tech industry, goes on to explore the prospects for long-term development of new techniques to benefit the natural and social environment. This great labour was stimulated by the fear of retrenchment in the Aerospace industry, when Tony Benn invited the shop stewards at Lucas Aerospace to put forward proposals for alternative uses which could harness the skill and creativity of a workforce whose talents would otherwise be jettisoned on the scrapheap of already widespread unemployment.

Cooley's team of shop stewards deliberately designed their research to cause 'respondents to think of products not merely for their exchange value but for their use value'.

They collected a large number of proposals for new products, and grouped them into six major ranges containing technical details, economic calculations and even engineering drawings. They sought a mix of products, some of which would be profitable under market criteria and some of which might not necessarily be profitable 'but would be highly socially useful'. After encouraging this enormous effort by trade unionists, Tony Benn was unable to see it through to fruition because he was redeployed by Harold Wilson in a cabinet reshuffle following the referendum on British membership of the European Community. Benn's demotion took him off to exile in the Department of Energy, and gave the subjects of the Department of Industry into the care of Eric Varley, whose appetite for industrial democracy had already diminished somewhat since he tasted the fruits of office.

The Spokesman never abandoned its interest and concern for democratic reform, especially in the areas of industrial autocracy and dictatorship. But we also maintained a continuous interest in the question of peace and disarmament, on which we have chosen two of our articles to celebrate the launch and development of the campaign for European Nuclear Disarmament. We launched this campaign alongside Edward Thompson, Dan Smith, Mary Kaldor and nuclear disarmament veterans such as Peggy Duff and Bruce Kent.

It was agreed that the Russell Foundation should canvass European support for this appeal, with the aim of convening a representative European Conference or Convention. After vigorous preparations the first such Convention met in Brussels in 1982, and it was agreed to follow it with a second such Convention in Berlin the following year. Retrospectively we can see that this marked the high-water mark of the END campaign.

It brought together strong representation from all the peace movements and pacifist groupings, together with most of the main European left and centre left political parties. The German Social Democrats and Greens were powerfully represented, as were the Italian Communists, the Labour Party and a cross-section of Scandinavians. We received strong support from Alva Myrdal, the pioneering Minister for Disarmament in Sweden.

All this gave rise to profound misgivings in the Soviet Peace Committee which did not relish the success of another peace movement which was non-aligned. We have reproduced some of the salient papers which reflect this controversy.

In those far off days the Labour Party in Britain agreed for the simultaneous dissolution of the North Atlantic Treaty Organisation and the Warsaw Pact. The Warsaw Pact dissolved itself many years ago, but the North Atlantic Treaty still seeks to expand itself eastwards to the great distress of all those against whom it is directed. Even if it reached as far as Vladivostok we sometimes get the impression that it would need new outlaws to mobilise against. President Eisenhower was right to warn us against the Military Industrial Complex, of which Nato is the living embodiment. If we continue to generate another hundred numbers of this journal, while we have breath left, we shall resist these embodiments of militarism, and continue to devote our energies to laying the foundations of the peaceful commonwealth which will come into existence with the abolition of war.

* * *

Eppur si muove

Of course the struggle continues. Labouring to produce 100 numbers of *The Spokesman* has taught us that none of our institutions can be taken for granted. The advance of democracy, in particular, needs to be maintained vigorously, or it will go into retreat. Years ago, Eric Hobsbawm wrote a famous article: 'The Forward March of Labour Halted'. But he did not accurately diagnose what caused the arrest. Actually, the trade unions continued to grow long after Hobsbawm thought that they were becalmed. The growth of trade union membership represented a growth in the negative power of Labour. It could block measures which offended it, but found the initiation of positive change far more difficult. That is why the 1970s began with a resounding debate about industrial democracy, leading to the Bullock Report and proposals for reform. These were all negated by a Parliament jealous of its powers, and above all anxious not to use them. Had the unions been able to initiate positive changes, British history might have been completely different. But the defeat of this impulse led directly to Mrs Thatcher, mass unemployment, and the wholesale reduction of trade union influence. It also led to an abrogation of many traditional democratic checks and balances.

Today, a new crisis is on us, and there may be a new birth of trade union disquiet. Can this mutate into positive change? If it does not, the future may be dire.

Ken Coates

COMMUNICATION WORKERS UNION

End the occupation of Iraq and Afghanistan

Don't attack Iran

Billy Hayes
General Secretary

Davie Bowman
President

Russell as Industrial Democrat

Charles Atkinson and John Hughes

This paper was commissioned for a symposium published on Russell's centenary in 1972. Here it is slightly abridged. John Hughes, Principal of Ruskin College, was a founder member of the Institute for Workers' Control, with which Russell identified at the time of its formation in 1968.

The motive in exploring systematically Russell's views on socialism is to emphasise the continuing relevance of his views. Russell's writings on the subject – stretching over more than half a century – succeed in identifying the most critical problems both of theory and practice that beset socialist and labour movements. Moreover, there is a consistency and continuity of approach on his part that offers the material for a comprehensive view of what socialist objectives and labour movement practice should consist in …

… Russell, who perceived what one might call the Englishness of much of Marx's analysis of capitalist economic relationships, was himself very concerned with events and movements of thought in Britain. He was, alas, sufficiently influenced by Sidney Webb to become for a brief time 'an imperialist, and even supported the Boer war'.[1] But his acquaintance with the theorists and practitioners of state socialism in Britain does not seem to have modified his earlier critical reaction to the same phenomenon in Marxist philosophical clothing. It is clear from his writings that the emergence of syndicalist, and in Britain 'guild' socialist, ideas of socialism and of the strategy required to reach a socialist society greatly extended his critical response to the growing debate on socialism. He joined the Labour Party in 1914, but by then his positive views on socialism and 'social reconstruction' already form a systematic whole whose reach far distanced orthodox British socialism. In 1915 he was writing lectures that provided the gist of his analysis (subsequently published as *Principles of Social Reconstruction*); the same analysis recurs – but with much more detailed reference across to Marxist, anarchist, syndicalist and guild socialist schools of thought – in *Roads to Freedom,* which was written later on in the course of the First World War and completed just before the unfreedom of a period of imprisonment.

Subsequent studies, not least *The Practice and Theory of Bolshevism* and *The Prospects of Industrial Civilisation*, fill out Russell's mature view of society and of the special problems of socialism in 'undeveloped' countries. In view of the elements both of continuity and repetition in all these writings, and in subsequent ones, we have attempted to distil from them in brief form the main arguments that Russell was accepting from socialist thought and practice, and the main, critical and positive contribution he was himself making.

Russell's acceptance of the socialist critique of capitalism

It is clear how completely Russell accepted the main critical arguments that socialist thought directed against capitalism as a social and economic system. He also added additional elements of his own, He took over from *The Communist Manifesto* ('this magnificent work' he called it in his first book, even while he was sharply challenging many aspects of Marxist orthodoxy) the recognition of the destructive and dynamic drive of industrial capitalism; he took over from Marxism also the notion of the permanent importance and irreversible nature of the internal drive of capitalist enterprise to concentration of large-scale production and an ever extending integration of production processes. If anything he extended traditional socialism's view of the alienating, de-humanising, and destructive nature of capitalism. In its shortest expression Russell puts his view of capitalism:

> 'Except slavery, the present industrial system is the most destructive of life that has ever existed. Machinery and large-scale production are ineradicable, and must survive in any better system.' [2]

It is particularly important for an understanding of his positive views on socialism to notice the emphasis Russell placed on the denial of *initiative* under capitalism to most people. In this he echoes Marx's point in the *Manifesto* that capitalism has expropriated most people's *property*[3] but extends the point to emphasise the denial of a creative role in society:

> 'The chief defect of the present system is that work done for wages very seldom affords any outlet for the creative impulse. The man who works for wages has no choice as to what he shall make; the whole creativeness of the process is concentrated in the employer who orders the work to be done … the work becomes a merely external means to a certain result, the earning of wages … And so the process of production, which should form one instinctive cycle, becomes divided into separate purposes, which can no longer provide any satisfaction of instinct for those who do the work.'[4]

Beyond this, of course, Russell accepted the socialist argument that capitalism as a system of distribution denied any opportunity for justice and was 'indefensible from every point of view'. As he put it in a satirical passage:

> 'We may distinguish four chief sources of recognised legal rights to private property (1) a man's right to what he has made himself; (2) the right to interest on capital which has been lent; (3) the ownership of land; (4) inheritance. These form a crescendo of

respectability: capital is more respectable than labour, land is more respectable than capital, and any form of wealth is more respectable when it is inherited than when it has been acquired by our own exertions.'[5]

It reads as a very English comment directed at the aristocratic society from which Russell had disengaged himself. But his further criticism of the nature and direction of capitalism has a more universal significance, and raised sixty years ago the issue that modern critics of capitalism are increasingly emphasising.

As Russell put it, one of the least questioned assumptions of capitalism was that production ought to be increased by every possible means; this belief in the importance of production had 'a fanatical irrationality and ruthlessness':

'The purpose of maximizing production will not be achieved in the long run if our present industrial system continues. Our present system is wasteful of human material. The same is true of material resources; the minerals, the virgin forests, and the newly developed wheatfields of the world are being exhausted with a reckless prodigality which entails almost a certainty of hardship for future generations.'[6]

So, the final contradiction in capitalism is that in the name of 'growth' it strips and robs the human and material resources of the planet; the technical progress which is claimed as the contribution of capitalism operates within a destructive, robber economy which is bringing closer the prospect of decay and diminishing returns.[7]

The 'philosophy of life' which accompanies this worship of production is that what 'matters most to a man's happiness is his income', a philosophy says Russell that is harmful because

'it leads men to aim at a result rather than an activity, an enjoyment of material goods in which men are not differentiated, rather than a creative impulse which embodies each man's individuality.'[8]

We do not think that later socialist writings on the distorting and manipulating effects of capitalist organised consumption have improved on that sentence of Russell which embodies both his criticism of capitalism and his social goal.

Russell's critique of socialism

Russell did not move from acceptance of socialist criticism of capitalism (and his own further extension of that critique) to an acceptance of the social goals posed by the state socialists of his time. This arose partly from his sense of the *inadequacy* of socialist views of the principles and nature of a socialist society,[9] partly it arose from a much more specific concern as to the implications of the extended role of the state that orthodox socialism appeared to be stressing. This critique of state socialism is particularly important in understanding Russell's views on the political and economic development of the labour movement. For, as we shall see subsequently, the discussion of the *transition* to socialism posed for him not only the question of whether the agencies of social action and change could reach as far as the overcoming of capitalism, *but also* whether they offered a road to an adequate social system, to a socialism that would not contain its own seeds of degeneration and denial of human creativity.

In various ways Russell sought to emphasise the achievement of human creativity as a necessary ingredient for post-capitalist society: 'to promote all that is creative, and so to diminish the impulses and desires that centre round possession'.[10] His concern about the role of the state was linked to his identification of the state so far as the embodiment of possessive forces, both internally and externally, and to the coercive role of the state ('the repository of collective force'). Moreover he saw that a transfer of the property claims from the individual capitalist to the state could produce a perpetuation of the wages system, a kind of bureaucratised state capitalism. After the criticism of the wage-earner/employer relationship that was quoted earlier, he went on to say:

> 'This result is due to our industrial system, but it would not be avoided, by state socialism. In a socialist community, the state would be the employer, and the individual workman would have almost as little control over his work as he has at present. Such control as he could exercise would be indirect, through political channels, and would be too slight and roundabout to afford any appreciable satisfaction. It is to be feared that instead of an increase of self-direction, there would only be an increase of mutual interference.'[11]

That sounds all too accurately like an appraisal of British nationalised industries. His initial pessimistic view of the denial of creativity if state socialism produced an enforced discipline reads all too obviously like a prescient view of the Soviet Union, or Czechoslovakia, seventy-five years later:

> 'State socialism means an increase of the powers of absolutism and police rule, and … acquiescence in such a state, whatever bribes it may offer to labour, is acquiescence in the suppression of all free speech and all free thought, is acquiescence in intellectual stagnation and moral servility.'[12]

Russell's underlying argument is that there are four requirements for a humanly adequate industrial system, four tests which can be applied to actual or proposed systems. They are (i) the maximising of production, (ii) justice in distribution, (iii) a tolerable existence for producers, and (iv) 'the greatest possible freedom and stimulus to vitality and progress'. As we have seen, capitalism could only lay claim to an interest in the first of these goals, and in Russell's view would by its nature fail to achieve it and instead bequeath a robbed and stripped planet to future generations. State socialism aimed primarily at the second and third objective; that is, it concentrates on justice, on the removal of inequality. But, says Russell, while justice may be a necessary principle it is not a *sufficient* one on which to base a social reconstruction. In its assertion of justice 'the labour movement is morally irresistible … all living thought is on its side'. But, justice 'by itself, when once realised, contains no source of new life'.[13]

Russell's concern is twofold. Partly, that there are tendencies in the evolution of the labour movement (and in the resistance it has to overcome to achieve its objectives) that might make it repressive and hostile to 'the life of the mind'.[14]

(Interestingly, he is concerned that labour discipline and the requirement that all should contribute to society should not be pushed so far as to produce intolerance to those who might want to drop out, to make only a minimum contribution, in the pursuit of individual creativity). He is also concerned at the danger of conservatism in methods of production, since technical progress may involve permanent loss to wage-earners. But the way to overcome this, he argued, was to give to labour 'the direct interest in economical processes' which otherwise belongs to the employer, whether capitalist or state. The capitalist system has robbed most men of initiative; the danger of state socialism is that it might perpetuate this by taking over into the hands of a state bureaucracy the initiative, the power, and the autocracy that are the hallmarks of the industrial capitalist.

Russell does not seek to reduce the severity of the problem posed by the kind of retreat from large-scale industry that at least one school of British socialists had envisaged. We have seen that he postulates continued concentration of production into technically progressive large-scale industry. Instead he argues for the democratization of the industrial process:

> 'Economic organisations, in the pursuit of efficiency, grow larger and larger, and there is no possibility of reversing this process. The causes of their growth are technical, and large organisations must be accepted as an essential part of civilised society. But there is no reason why their government should be centralised and monarchical. The present economic system by robbing most men of initiative, is one of the causes of the universal weariness which devitalises urban and industrial populations … If we are to retain any capacity for new ideas … the monarchical organisation of industry must be swept away. All large businesses must become democratic and federal in their government. The whole wage-earning system is an abomination, not only because of the social injustice which it causes and perpetuates, but also because it separates the man who does the work from the purpose for which the work is done.'[15]

So, 'industrial federal democracy' is the direction that has to be taken to reconstruct the industrial system. Industrial capitalism has separated the several interests of consumer, producer, capitalist, and the community. Co-operative systems offer some link between consumer and capitalist; syndicalism offers a link between producer and capital. No form of organisation links all these interests and makes them quite identical with the community's interest. Russell, in other words, envisages a pluralist society of participating democracies, although recognising that this still leaves the need to harmonise these differing organisations with their separate initiatives. The state appears, in this approach, as arbitrator and co-ordinator.

One advantage of this perspective is, as Russell puts it, that 'it is not a static or final system: it is hardly more than a framework for energy and initiative'. It offers the greater flexibility of combining geographical units of government with industrial democracies whose constituencies are trades and industries. Such an approach clearly begins to raise in a relevant way a socialist view of the future of what are already multi-national enterprises, and the need for an international as well as national framework for socialist societies. The sources of creative initiative are multiplied in such federal and democratic framework; the opportunities for voluntary membership of industrial organisation, instead of legal or economic compulsion,[16] are enhanced.

It becomes obvious at this point, that Russell is not only depicting the dynamic framework required for a creative form of socialism. He is also arguing for the development of this organisational base, particularly the development of the federal democracy of trade unions with an increased emphasis on encroaching control, as the way to strengthen the democratic and labour movement under capitalism. He is writing both about a socialism that does not rest on the worship of state power, and about the 'roads to freedom', about the transition to socialism. He is writing about a creative and dynamic form of socialism but also about the way to create a dynamic for change within capitalism. We need, therefore, to look more systematically at Russell's critical appraisal of the operational experience of labour movements, and at his views of the organisational and policy requirements that these movements expressed.

Russell's views on the transition to socialism

The conventional argument within the labour movement over several generations has been between reformist and revolutionary modes of progression. The concealed assumption, which Russell was critical of from the beginning, was the emphasis on political party organisation and activity and the devaluing of the role of trade union and industrial action. Russell's analysis – both of German social democracy in its early days and of Lenin's views – makes it clear that instead of Communist Party organisation in the advanced countries developing as the revolutionary polar opposite of earlier reformism, it tended to reproduce the oscillation between ostensible revolutionary ideology and practical ineffectiveness and political accommodation that he found in Germany in the 1890s. In our view, Russell offers the clues for a major reconsideration of the development of labour and socialist movements; the flaw in the pattern of socialist response Russell traced back to Marx himself. The outturn, as it appears to us, is either political compromise within advanced capitalist systems increasingly having recourse to a state apparatus with what one might call Bismarckian tendencies, or political revolution in less developed countries in periods of social breakdown with the likely outturn of a repressive state 'socialism'.

Russell saw the transition to socialism as a compelling problem because it was not *simply* a matter of superseding capitalism; it was not true that we could rely on 'living happily ever after' by whatever road we came. There was also involved the wider struggle between the creative needs of humanity and the complex and potentially coercive nature of modern large-scale production (which, remember, Russell saw as common both to advanced capitalism and to post-capitalist society). The double requirement, to ask of socialist movements, therefore, was that they should be capable of transforming society instead of getting trapped *in* some accommodation within capitalism, and that they should at least begin to reflect the organization and attitudes needed to humanise the industrial society of the future.

It was therefore of the utmost importance for Russell that socialists followed a course that led to the actual liberation of man, not 'proletarian revenge':

> 'While I am as convinced a socialist as the most ardent Marxian, I do not regard socialism as a gospel of proletarian revenge, nor even *primarily* as a means of securing economic justice. I regard it primarily as an adjustment to machine production demanded primarily by considerations of common sense, and calculated to increase the happiness not only of proletarians, but of all except a tiny minority of the human race!'[17]

Nor should the labour movement follow a course that produced a type of economic justice superimposed on the fabric of an authoritarian state.[18]

Russell's first study of social democracy in Germany is relevant because for the first time he begins to express the nature of his concern about the transition as well as making a penetrating criticism of the philosophy and tactics of the most powerful political labour movement at that time (the 1890s).[19] The Social Democrats were directly dependent on Marx's analysis and ideology and were agitating for socialism in an industrially advanced (at least, rapidly advancing) country. Russell criticised the Social Democrats for dogmatically adhering to tenets of Marx some of which he thought held little validity for Germany at the time. More particularly he felt that they had uncritically accepted and then made more rigid Marx's views on wages. Lassalle indeed injected into German Social Democracy his so-called 'Iron Law' of wages – what one might call an ultra-pessimistic view of the scope for trade union economic pressure. Russell unfortunately sometimes seems to transfer this rigid notion from Lassalle to Marx.

> 'The Iron Law has for the moment a certain amount of validity. Marx's doctrines have therefore a sufficient kernel of truth to make them seem self-evident to German workmen. It is unfortunate, however, that their apparent necessity, under a capitalistic regime, should make German labourers very lukewarm as to trade union and all non-political means of improving their condition. The exclusively political character of Social Democracy, which is mainly due to Marx, is thus of very doubtful validity.'[20]

As early as 1896, then, Russell foresaw a distinctive role for unions in the development of a viable transition to socialism, and later he was to fault Lenin for his inability to comprehend the potential power of trade unions. Russell's point is *both* that there may be distinct gains in terms of real wages and conditions to be secured from strong trade unions, *and* that the organisational experience (as he would have later put it, of 'federal democracy') and ability to advance the frontier of unionised control were additional gains of lasting significance.[21] If, Russell felt, the trade unions were under-valued as a force for change, then the ability of the predominantly political-party organisation to break through beyond capitalism was reduced, and there might be little hope for the extended role of trade unions as an independent source of social initiative after any successful revolution, because the orthodox Marxist approach would invite greatly increased state power, would emerge as state socialism.

The view implicit in this, and advanced by Russell with more confidence once syndicalist and guild socialist ideas became influential, is that a programme for the transition to socialism had to overcome the limitations of state socialism not least by acknowledging an extended role for trade unions.

Meanwhile, the Social Democrats, in Russell's view, were in difficulties in developing a coherent policy that attracted a mass base. On the one hand, recognition of gradations in class structure and the political attitudes of different social groups[22] were causing the German Social Democrats to 'revise their beliefs and to adopt an evolutionary rather than revolutionary attitude ... Such doctrines diminish revolutionary ardour and tend to transform socialists into a left wing of the Liberal. Party.'[23] On the other hand, the ruling class were able to separate them from the general public, mobilising 'popular enmity' against them by a distorted projection of their revolutionary philosophy and aspirations:

'When a party proclaims class-warfare as its fundamental principle, it must expect the principle to be taken up by the classes against which its war is directed. But the popular enmity which was necessary to the passing of the Law,[24] though in large measure due to misrepresentation of bourgeois press and bourgeois politicians, was also, and principally, a religious antagonism to the new philosophy of life which Marxianism had introduced.'[25]

In fact, this combination of practical ineffectiveness and accommodation within the system together with an ostensible revolutionary philosophy and purpose seems to have dogged both social democratic and communist parties within advanced capitalist countries. In diluted form what was true of German social democracy in the 1890s appears relevant to the successive political failures of the British Labour Party, or is exemplified, too, in the French Communist Party.

Russell saw the need to remove the 'popular enmity' that reaction could mobilise against the socialist and labour movement, and to secure instead a mass base of popular support as the guarantee for a successful revolution. He was deeply conscious of the risks involved in an all out revolutionary confrontation in advanced countries:

'What was true of the late war' (ie, 1914-18) 'would be true in a far higher degree of a universal class war, because it would be longer, more desperate, and of greater extent. It may be taken as nearly certain that such a war would not end in the establishment of either capitalism or socialism, since both are forms of industrialism and both depend upon the existence of a more or less civilised community.'[26]

Hence his emphasis on the need for popular support for a transition to socialism, and his recoil from revolutionary adventurism. His view was that political revolution was in fact less likely in the advanced countries and the opportunities greater in less developed ones, but this again led to further problems of the post-revolutionary transition.

In the specific case of Russia, Russell was conscious of the inadequacies of the Bolshevik programme. The continuous civil war and near world war after revolution brought about extreme poverty and the inability to inculcate

Communist ideals, and the seriousness of this situation led to the establishment of a despotic bureaucracy that could only be removed by a new revolution. The seizure of power by a few guaranteed the separation of these men from the genuine proletarian, and hence was the origin of a new ruling class. Russell did not believe that the Bolshevik model would produce the socialism that the Bolsheviks earlier aspired to.

The shock of this recognition was so great that Russell comments:

> 'My first impulse was to abandon political thinking as a bad job, and to conclude that the strong and reckless must always exploit the weaker and kindlier sections of the population.'[27]

Fortunately, hope and intellectual resilience being stronger, Russell continued to try to analyse the faults in the Bolshevik model.[28] He decided that the concentration on economic inequality, while accurate, avoided a problem of equal magnitude – the inequality of power. (As we have seen, in his writing during the First World War, Russell had seen this as a critical weakness in state socialism; thus he was not unprepared intellectually for this outcome).

Perhaps, Russell reasoned in *The Prospects of Industrial Civilisation*, the failure of the Bolsheviks was also connected with their attempt 'to establish communism in a country almost untouched by capitalist industrialism', thus raising the question of whether capitalism is a necessary stage on the road to socialism or whether industry can be developed 'socialistically from the outset in a hitherto undeveloped country'. Significantly, he added that this was a question of vital importance 'for the future of Russia and Asia'.[29]

The undeveloped countries, in Russell's view, have one major advantage in any attempted transition, favourable political conditions – they do not have a ruling élite of powerful capitalists, and their wage earners are not so bemused as the workers in advanced countries who 'continue to elect as their chosen representatives men whose delight it is to oppress, starve and imprison all who advocate the interests of the wage-earners'.[30] But technical and economic conditions are a distinct disadvantage. The needed accumulation of capital seems to require that industrialism must be autocratically governed, and provide bare subsistence wages. Foreign capital and technology may also be important for an undeveloped country, and this interference by foreign capitalists leads to 'loopholes for corruption'. Moreover, even if revolutionary ardour suffices during the first militant phase of the transition, the second 'constructive' phase is very long, and the revolutionary zeal will diminish. Pessimistically, Russell concludes:

> 'there is, it would seem, only one force which could keep communism up to the necessary pitch of enthusiasm, and that is nationalism developing into imperialism as foreign aggressions are defeated.'[31]

Nevertheless, Russell conceded the possibility that the Bolsheviks might succeed, and 'if they do, they may quite possibly become a model for China and India'. Another possibility was that of the Russian state replacing the foreign capitalist as the exploiter; what Russell here envisages is Russia playing the role of provider of capital, goods, and technology to these countries in a state capitalist form, and help these countries to 'escape ... private capitalism'.[32]

Thus the cumulative problems of a political revolution as a major element in the transition to socialism were seen by Russell as the risk of material devastation, the special and protracted problems of an economic transition for undeveloped countries which offered the best hope of political transition, and the likelihood that these conditions would result in the wielding of power through a state bureaucracy with a resulting repression of human creativity.

Russell's main hope of a transition to socialism therefore remained based on the possibilities within advanced countries, where the technical and economic conditions were most favourable, and combined with a wage-earning class not only educated and accustomed to industrial processes, but also capable of more developed trade union organisation. But this is to come back to the question of how to break out beyond the confined achievement of traditional political social democracy (and the latter-day repetition of the same process through traditional communist party activity).

Russell's central idea is the importance to be attached to a persistent extension of the scope and direction of trade union organisation and power. The under-valuing of trade union organisation was one of the main criticisms directed at the German Social Democrats. It was the injection of this idea of the potential sweep of trade unionism in transforming industrial society – rather than the practicality of particular methods proposed – that he held to be the permanent achievement of syndicalism:

> 'There is no doubt that the ideas which it' (i.e. syndicalism) 'has put into the world have done a great deal to revive the Labour Movement and to recall it to certain things of fundamental importance which it had been in danger of forgetting. Syndicalists consider man as producer rather than consumer. They are more concerned to procure freedom in work than to increase material well-being. They have revived the quest for liberty, which was growing somewhat dimmed under the regime of parliamentary socialism, and they have reminded men that what our modern society needs is not a little tinkering here and there, nor the kind of miner readjustments to which the existing holders of power may readily consent, but a fundamental reconstruction, a sweeping away of all the sources of oppression, a liberation of men's constructive energies, and a wholly new way of conceiving and regulating production and economic relations. This merit is so great that, in view of it, all minor defects become insignificant, and this merit syndicalism will continue to possess even if, as a definite movement, it should be found to have passed away with the war.'[33]

The sympathy that breathes through this passage is evident, and indeed the change of tone in the discussion of socialism as between the writing of *German Social Democracy* and the books he was writing from 1915 onwards seems to owe much to the increased confidence that a more realistic 'road to freedom' was being depicted, one that would be capable of leading to a humanised industrial society.

Thus, on one side, Russell defended syndicalism against the criticisms of would-be revolutionary anarchism with its emphasis on the need for 'armed insurrection and violent appropriation':

'Syndicalists might retort that when the movement is strong enough to win by armed insurrection it will be abundantly strong enough to win by the General Strike. In Labour movements generally, success through violence can hardly be expected except in circumstances where success without violence is attainable.'[34]

Russell's view is that better trade union organisation can establish the power base needed to ensure that the rights of labour are respected and to extend labour's economic control.[35] Trade unionism and the accompanying reasoned propaganda of socialist opinion must not only win over 'the less well-paid industrial workers'. In addition:

'It is necessary to win over the technical staff ... It is necessary to win over a considerable proportion of the professional classes and of the intellectuals.'[36]

Socialists, he says, have been 'too impatient' and this has inspired their emphsis on force instead of reason, and on 'the dictatorship of the communist party'. But if 'all who will really profit by socialism have become persuaded of the fact' the force needed to take the capital from the capitalists 'will be only a very little force'.

Moreover, trade unionism has been moving in the right direction in establishing increased control over work processes in ways which directly challenge the repressive production-worshipping values of capitalism:

'The first steps towards a cure for these evils are being taken by the trade unions, in those parts of their policy which are most criticised, such as restriction of output, refusal to believe that the only necessity is more production, shortening of hours ... It is only by these methods that industrialism can be humanized ... It could be used to lighten physical labour, and to set men free for more agreeable activities ... The trade unions have clearly perceived this, and have persisted in spite of lectures from every kind of middle and upper-class pundit. This is one reason why there is more hope from self-government in industry than from State Socialism.'[37]

Nor was Russell to be turned aside from this belief by the repudiation of self-government in industry by the Bolsheviks; they were opposing self-government in industry everywhere because it had failed in Russia and their self-esteem prevented them admitting that this was due to backwardness:

'I would go so far as to say that the winning of self-government in such industries as railways and mining is an essential preliminary to complete Communism. In England, especially, this is the case. Trade unions can command whatever technical skill they may require; they are politically powerful; the demand for self-government is one for which there is widespread sympathy ... moreover (what is important with the British temperament) self-government can be brought about gradually by stages in each trade, and by extension from one trade to another.'[38]

This broad sympathy of Russell for the advocates of self-government in industry shows through in his extensive discussion of Guild Socialist ideas (particularly in

Roads to Freedom). However, he did not believe that the Guild Socialists had in any way solved the problem of the institutional form that decision making, and the relations between 'self-governing' industries and the state, would take.[39] He thought also that they misrepresented in suggesting that the state would be the repository of consumer interests as against the producer interests centred in the guilds. 'Neither the interests of the producer, nor those of the consumer, can be adequately represented except by ad hoc organizations ... If capitalism were eliminated, the political strength of production as against consumption might be greatly increased. If so, the need of organising consumers to protect their own interest would become greater'.[40]

The warning seems justified, though the ever-more evident social costs attaching to capitalist production, the rapid emergence of major problems of ecology and pollution, may well be providing the stimulus that will accelerate the development of consumer interests and the greater recognition of these by local and national (and international?) government.

Russell clearly sees the extension of trade union organization and power, its developing interest in control, its assertion of a human scale of values, as critically important for the transition to socialism in mature countries. We should remember, though, that this is to him part of a more general advocacy of a pluralism of voluntary and autonomous organizations, acting as centres of creative initiative; that is, federal and democratic trade unionism is part of his general view of the structure of a democratic society:

'It is not only geographical units, such as nations, that have a right, according to the true theory of democracy, to autonomy for certain purposes. Just the same principle applies to any group which has important internal concerns that affect the members of the group enormously more than they affect outsiders. The theory of democracy ... demands (1) division of the community into more or less autonomous groups; (2) delimitation of the powers of the autonomous groups by determining which of their concerns are so much more important to themselves than to others that others had better have no say in them ... In an ideal democracy, industries ... would be self-governing as regards almost everything except the price and quantity of their product ... Measures which they would then be able to adopt autonomously they are now justified in extorting from the Government by direct action.'[41]

In a way, Russell's long-term belief in the reasonableness of his view of the progress of industrial society to communism is derived – as was Marx's – from a sense of the incompatability between private property claims (with a legal form relevant to a predominantly agrarian and handicraft economy) and the more and more extensive co-operation of productive forces required by modern industrial society.[42] Looked at in that way, it is the capitalist form of industrial society that is temporary:

'Capitalism is essentially transitional, the survival of private property in the means of production into the industrial era, which has no place for it owing to the fact that production has become co-operative. Capitalism, by being ill adapted to industrialism, rouses an opposition which must in the end destroy it. The only question is whether labour will be strong enough to establish socialism upon the ruins of capitalism, or whether capitalism will be able to destroy our whole industrial civilization in the course of the struggle ...'[43]

Reading Russell, one is struck, time and again, with his remarkable predictive abilities, his power of constructing an analysis of social and economic processes that describe with great accuracy the movement of history after he has written. That he bears comparison with Marx in this respect is no mere accident.

Russell was able to use his critical understanding of Marx to penetrate and comprehend the complex class and power relationships created by the development of capitalism; this understanding extended to the processes as they would affect undeveloped countries as well as the advanced industrial countries.

His analysis served a twofold purpose; first to inject the dialectic of social process with a new life, and give it more humanized form. Secondly, to give a direction to those processes that might break through the capitalist integument of industrial society – its values as well as its property relationships. Echoing Marx's *Economic and Philosophic Manuscripts of 1844*,[44] but in a far less abstract manner, Russell attempted to analyse the positive effects of industrialism. If wage-earners (and by extension, technical and professional workers) could gain control of the productive apparatus, then they could use the efficiency of the process for the development of human creativity. Through group autonomy and collective control the de-humanising aspects of the process could be overcome – partially even within capitalism, and completely after its demise (to which this control contributes).

Russell once commented that Marx was 'the last of the great system builders', but it is Russell's analysis of the whole process involved in the evolution of industrial society, not simply the economic process, that enabled him to be so prescient. Like Marx, there is tremendous consistency in the structure of his ideas, but like Marx we have to cull these from the writings of a lifetime. Like Marx, Russell's concern is with 'real men' in their real social and material relationships, and it was this concern that led him to regard authoritarian power structures as anathema to the development of the creative powers of man.

Hence his persistent criticisms of state socialism as the social goal, and his critical attack on representative formal political democracy as an inadequate defence against autocracy and the centralization of power. Participatory democracy, based particularly on trade unions and other functional organizations, is, in Russell's view, the way to release men's energy and creativity, the road to the harmonisation of the industrial system and its requirements with human needs, the 'road to freedom'.

Footnotes

1. B. Russell, 'My Mental Development', from *The Philosophy of Bertrand Russell*, sel. By P.A. Schilpp, 1951, reprinted in *The Basic Writings of Bertrand Russell*, ed. by R.E. Egner & LE. Denonn, 1961.

2. *Principles of Social Reconstruction*, p.244.

3. *The Communist Manifesto*: 'You are horrified at our intending to do away with private property. But in your existing society, private property is already done away with for nine-tenths of the population; its existence for the few is solely due to its non-existence in the hands of those nine-tenths.'

4. *Principles of Social Reconstruction*, p.136.

5. *Op. cit.* p.123.

6. *0p. cit.* p.123.

7. Besides, says Russell, the greater productivity arising from industrialism has 'enabled us to devote more labour and capital to armies and navies for the protection of our wealth from envious neighbours, and for the exploitation of inferior races, which are ruthlessly wasted by the capitalist regime,' *Op. cit.* p.119.

8. *Op. cit.* p.244.

9. Russell is scathing about 'the old type of Marxian revolutionary socialist' who never dwelt on the life of communities after the 'millennium': 'He imagined that, like the prince and princess in a fairy story, they would live happily ever after.'

10. *Op. cit.* p.236.

11. *Op. cit.* p.137.

12. *German Social Democracy*, pp.113-114. See also, *Roads to Freedom* (1966 edn.) p.91-92: 'State socialists argue as if there would be no danger to liberty in a State not based on capitalism. This seems to me an entire delusion.' Russell's argument rests in part on what he sees as inherent defects in the working of *representative* (as against more participatory) democratic institutions; cf. *Roads to Freedom*, p.93.

13. *Principles of Social Reconstruction*, pp.123-131.

14. This is expressed also in *Roads to Freedom*, where on pages 79 and 80 he expresses his fears of orthodox socialism, and in Ch.VIII ('Science and Art under Socialism') argues for tolerance for creative activity.

15. *Op. cit.* p.138.

16. *Op, cit.* p.139-142. 'If organisation is not to crush individuality, membership of an organisation ought to be voluntary, not compulsory, and ought always to carry with it a voice in the management.'

17. Essay on 'The Case for Socialism', in *In Praise of Idleness* (first publ. 1935), 1970 edn. p.76.

18. Russell did not assume that the Russian revolution must of necessity lead to that. On his early hopes see *The Prospects of Industrial Civilisation*, 1923, p.8.

19. Subsequently, of course, Michels quarried in the same place. Although Russell grasped the oligarchical degeneration of representative political organisation and processes that Michels emphasised, Michels never appears to have seen the even more vital points that Russell goes on to make. Astonishingly, Michels in *Political Parties* shows no sign of knowing – he certainly does not refer to – Russell's work.

20. *German Social Democracy*, 1896, pp.27-28.

21. In 1923 he wrote: 'The iron law of wages, invented by orthodox economists to discourage trade unions, and accepted by Marx to encourage revolution, was an economic fallacy.' (*Prospects of Industrial Civilisation*, pp.105-106) This aphorism of Russell's distorts Marx's views, although it is quite accurate when applied to most of the German 'marxists' at the time in question. Marx in fact combined pessimism about the possible economic achievements of trade unionism with understanding of the wider importance of their persistent organisation: 'Now and then the workers are victorious,

but only for a time. The real fruit of their battle lies not in the immediate result but in the ever expanding union of the workers,' but then by a curious elision goes on: 'This organisation of the proletarians into a class, and consequently into a political party ... ' (*The Communist Manifesto*).

22. *Roads to Freedom*, pp34-35.
23. *Op. cit.* p.35
24. The 'Exceptional Law' which had deprived socialists of many of their rights.
25. *German Social Democracy*, pp.92-93.
26. *The Prospects of Industrial Civilisation*, p.128. See also *The Communist Manifesto*, 'The history of all hitherto existing society is the history of class struggles ... a fight that each time ended either in a revolutionary reconstruction of society at large, or in the common ruin of the contending classes.'
27. *Practice and Theory of Bolshevism*, 1920, p.157.
28. Russell saw this evaluation as imperative because: 'The civilised world seems almost certain, sooner or later, to follow the example of Russia in attempting a communist organisation of society. I believe that the attempt is essential to the happiness of mankind during the next few centuries, but I believe also that the transition has appalling dangers ... in the interests of communism, no less than in the interests of civilisation, I think it imperative that the Russian failure should be admitted and analysed.' *Practice and Theory of Bolshevism*, 1920, p.135.
29. *Prospects of Industrial Civilisation*, pp.106-107.
30. *Ibid.,* p.119.
31. *The Prospects of Industrial Civilisation*, p.117.
32. *Ibid.,* p.113.
33. *Roads to Freedom*, pp.66-67.
34. *Op. cit.* p.60.
35. *Prospects of Industrial Civilisation*, pp.240-241.
36. *Ibid.,* pp.138-139.
37. *Prospects of Industrial Civilisation*, p.175.
38. *Practice and Theory of Bolshevism*, pp.182-183.
39. *Roads to Freedom*, pp.94-95.
40. *Prospects of Industrial Civilisation*, p.238.
41. 'Democracy and Direct Action', 1919, reprinted in *The Spokesman*, No.22, April 1972.
42. This emphasis on the total productive process as the co-operative production of wealth seems to be the main force behind Russell's criticism of Marx's labour theory of value, or of the equivalent emphasis of pre-Marxist socialists on 'a man's right to the produce of his own labour'. This could not be used as 'the basis of a just system of distribution' says Russell for 'in the complication of modem industrial processes it is impossible to say what a man has produced'. (*Principles of Social Reconstruction*, p.124, and *German Social Democracy*, p.17).
43. *The Prospects of Industrial Civilisation*, pp. 62-63.
44. We are not implying that Russell used the *Manuscripts*, we have found no evidence that he used them (they were not published until 1932).

The Infancy of Socialism

Bertrand Russell

Russell's review of the first volume of Max Beer's A History of British Socialism *was published in* The Athenaeum *in 1919. This first volume of Beer's* History, *with its introduction by R.H. Tawney, was republished by Spokesman in an illustrated edition in 1984 (price £11.95, available from www.spokesmanbooks.com)*

This is an extraordinarily good book, the outcome of many years of patient research. Mr. Tawney's Introduction informs us that the second volume was nearly completed at the outbreak of the war, and will, it is hoped, appear on the return of peace. Mr. Beer has performed a labour of love in rescuing the work of many British pioneers from the oblivion to which the carelessness of their countrymen would confine them. 'From the thirteenth century to the present day,' he says, 'the stream of Socialism and social reform has largely been fed by British thought and experiment. Medieval schoolmen and statesmen, modern political philosophers, economists, poets and philanthropists of the British Isles have explored its course and enriched its volume, but left it to writers of other nations to name and describe it.' His preface, evidently written before the outbreak of the war, takes a view of our mental character which is flattering and somewhat unusual:

'The English intellect, from its sheer recklessness, is essentially revolutionary, probably more so than the French intellect. But since 1688 it has been the endeavour of English statesmen and educators to impart to the nation a conservative, cautiously moving temper, a distrust of generalisation, an aversion from carrying theory to its logical conclusions ... In periods of general upheavals, however, when the dynamic forces of society are vehemently asserting themselves, the English are apt to throw their mental ballast overboard and take the lead in revolutionary thought and action. In such a period we are living now.'

The first and shorter Part of this book deals with medieval ideas and their collapse, down to the year 1760. Mr. Beer complains of the lack of a book on the English schoolmen, of whose political ideas he gives a concise account. We wonder how many of the inhabitants of the village of Ockham are aware that it gave its name to one of the great minds of the world. Mr. Beer suggests that perhaps Hales, Duns Scotus and Ockham are regarded as foreigners because the first died at Paris, the second at Cologne, and the third at Munich'. Duns Scotus has left no trace in the national life beyond the word 'dunce' – a warning to philosophers as to what the English think of thought.

It is and always has been the practice of the human race to put to death those who first advocate the ideas which are afterwards found most conducive to the welfare of mankind. About half the pioneers mentioned in this book were executed by due process of law; most of the rest underwent long terms of imprisonment. We learn, incidentally, that an ancestor of Keir Hardie was hanged for high treason in 1820 because he advocated a general strike for the purpose of obtaining universal suffrage.

The book is a history of ideas rather than of political movements. The ideas that underlie Socialism are explicit in More's Utopia, and Mr. Beer shows that they were common among men of learning throughout the Middle Ages. What makes the political difference between one age and another is not the ideas of the thoughtful minority, but the occupations and economic interests of the ordinary men and women. The fact that Socialism is no longer a speculation of the few, but a powerful force capable of dethroning monarchs and altering the constitution of society, is due to the progress of economic, political and military organization. The ideas of the schoolmen were inherited by the extremists of the Civil War, who were the first in England to form groups for the purpose of carrying out communism. Throughout almost the whole period dealt with in this volume, communistic groups were too weak numerically to aim at altering the State. The Diggers of 1649, who set to work to dig up and cultivate St. George's Hill near Esher in a spirit of Christian communism, may be regarded as initiating the long series of attempts to found small societies on ideal lines in the midst of an unregenerate environment. They preached and practised non-resistance, and Cromwell had no difficulty in suppressing them. It is surprising how long Socialists continued to believe in the usefulness of separate little colonies of the elect cut off from the general life of the world. And even now there are those who imagine that there can be victorious national Socialism while other nations adhere to the capitalist regime. The doctrine of the inevitable unity of the world is hard for impatient reformers, but those who forget it are doomed to futility. The very progress of industrialism which has caused the spread of Socialism has also made the world an economic whole, and swept away the former independence of the separate nations.

The second Part of Mr. Beer's book begins with the economic revolution, and closes with the era of disappointment after the passing of the Reform Bill. His summary of the period preceding the Reform Bill agitation is so admirable that we shall quote it as a sample of many others:

> 'From a sociological point of view, the period from 1760 to 1825 exhibits four phases. The first phase was purely parliamentary and constitutional; its protagonists, Wilkes and 'Junius', fought against the oligarchy and the remnants of personal monarchy; this phase is outside the plan of our work. The second phase was mainly agrarian; the effects of the rapid rate of enclosing farms and commons as well as of the improvements in agriculture turned the attention of revolutionary minds toward agrarian reform; its writers were Spence,

Ogilvie and Paine. The third phase was caused by enthusiasm for the French Revolution on the part of English intellectuals and London artizans, whose minds had been prepared by the theories which were current in the antecedent two phases; its writers were William Godwin, the youthful Coleridge, Southey, Wordsworth and John Thelwall. The fourth phase was that of the industrial revolution proper, the first critical writer of which was Charles Hall, followed by Robert Owen and his school, and the anti-capitalist critics, Ravenstone, Hodgskin, and several anonymous writers; the poet of this phase was Shelley. The common basis of all those writers consisted mainly of natural law as they found it in Locke's 'On Civil Government'. This small treatise became their Bible, particularly after its theories had been consecrated by the success of the American Revolution, and had come back to England from France endowed with the fiery soul of Rousseau.

The first use of the word 'Socialist', we are told, is in 1827, in the *Cooperative Magazine,* an Owenite publication. The word meant at that time an Owenite cooperator, not what it has since come to mean. Owen's influence is powerfully felt throughout the movements dealt with in the later chapters of the book, and its strength is shown in the opposition which Owen was able to maintain against the doctrine of the class-war, which became prevalent in Labour circles after the passing of the Reform Bill. Socialism in a more modern sense arose, as an economic theory, largely out of Ricardo's doctrine that labour is the measure of value. Mr. Beer maintains that most of the controversies promoted in Germany by Marx's *Capital* were fought out in essence in England between 1820 and 1830, and he gives an excellent account of the more or less Socialist writers who based themselves upon Ricardo – Thompson, Hodgskin, Ravenstone and the rest. We think, however, that he somewhat over-estimates these writers as compared with their continental successors. He himself points out that their criticism of capitalist society was made largely from the point of view of those who simply regretted the growth of industrialism and failed to see what was progressive in capitalism. In this respect Marx, with his conceptions of necessary epochs in economic development, and his realization of the revolutionary achievements of capitalism as against the old order, is immeasurably superior in intellectual power to any of his English precursors. One cannot say of him, what Mr. Beer truly says *à propos* of the British Socialists of the '20s, that

'Most writers on subjects of moral philosophy, social and economic science, and the history of nations, form their conception not from phenomena which are in the process of shaping themselves, but from phenomena which already belong to the past.'

This observation, we fear, has been true of the immense majority of philosophers, ever since Aristotle failed to notice the doings of Philip and Alexander. It will always be true of men whose ideas are derived from books and 'culture' rather than from contact with men and affairs.

In some ways the most interesting chapters in the book are the last three, which deal with the rise of Chartism, the alliance of Labour with the middle class in the fight for the Reform Bill, and their separation after it was found that the Bill had done nothing for the working class. Chartism had all the characteristics, except experience, that mark a modern Labour movement, including the doctrine of the class-war, and the conflict as to political and industrial methods. Its chief organ, the *Poor Man's Guardian,* defied the stamp-tax to which all newspapers were liable, and appeared at a penny, with the announcement on each number: 'Established contrary to Law to try the power of Might against Right'. Nowadays such a contest would be quickly decided, but in those times the State was less powerful or less determined. The *Poor Man's Guardian* was closely connected with 'The London National Union of the Working Classes', founded in 1831, a body of great importance in the history of Socialist ideas. Starting from Owenism, it gave rise to the Chartist movement and to discussions in which such modern policies as Syndicalism were (except in name) invented and first advocated. A good deal of what Mr. Beer has to tell concerning these discussions is, so far as we know, new, and some of it is surprising. It appears, for example, that in 1833, twenty-six years before the *Origin of Species,* meetings of working men were discussing the 'Simian hypothesis' that men were descended from the lower animals.

Coming to matters more nearly allied to Socialism, we find an account of William Benbow, the inventor of the general strike as a method of changing the economic constitution of society. His pamphlet on the subject bore the attractive title: *Grand National Holiday and Congress of the Productive Classes.* Every working-class family was to lay in a store of food, and stop work for a month: the month was to be devoted to concerting unity of action in the future and to devising the best constitution of society. The actual phrase 'general strike' was not used by Benbow, but was adopted by the trade unions, and is found as early as 1834. In these years, 1832-34, the trade unions were Syndicalist in outlook. They had been induced to support the Reform Bill, but the outcome had disgusted them with political methods. The degree to which modern ideas were anticipated is shown, for example, in an article in the *Crisis* (April 12, 1834) containing such passages as:

> 'We have never yet had a House of Commons. The only House of Commons is a House of Trades, and that is only just beginning to be formed. We shall have a new set of boroughs when the unions are organised: every trade shall be a borough, and every trade shall have a council of representatives to conduct its affairs.'

But the movement was short-lived. There was a general collapse in working-class movements in 1834, with which Mr. Beer's first volume ends. Every student of the history of ideas must earnestly hope that nothing will happen to prevent the publication of the second volume. It would be difficult to imagine a book more fair-minded than Mr. Beer's, or showing more mastery of the voluminous material of his subject. In spite of his great erudition, he never loses himself in detail, but shows himself at his best in his general summaries. In conclusion, we wish to associate ourselves with some wise words of Mr. Tawney's:

> 'At a time when to speak of the unity of Europe seems a cruel jest, a work like that of Mr. Beer, the history by an Austrian scholar of the English contribution to an international movement, is not only a valuable addition to historical knowledge, but a reminder that there are intellectual bonds which preceded the war and will survive it.'

Market against Environment

Karl W Kapp

Professor K. W. Kapp, the author of the classic work on The Social Costs of Business Enterprise, *(formerly* Capitalist Enterprise)*, was one of the foremost authorities on the economics of pollution and environmental control. This paper was first delivered at a Metalworkers' conference in 1972, and published in* The Spokesman *as one of the main documents for the first conference on Socialism and the Enviromment, which was convened by the Russell Foundation. This led directly to the establishment of the Socialist Environmental and Resources Association (SERA), which continues to this day. The article was first published in* Spokesman 23, *in 1972.*

Since the Second World War the disruption of the natural and social environment, especially in the industrialised countries, has proceeded at an accelerating pace. If the deterioration of the quality of life could be quantified, it could probably be shown to be intensifying at a far higher rate than increases in population or GNP. In Tokyo it has already become necessary to install automatic warning systems which halt production temporarily in those firms whose waste products contain highly dangerous materials, and the population is discouraged from physical exertion at times of extreme air pollution.[1]

It is no coincidence that the intensification in pollution should occur at this time – for scientific research and the development of new, untested technologies have reached such proportions that their effects determine the quality of life. The systematisation of the theory of management and operational research, both in the private and public sector, will hardly be able to stop this process. I shall attempt to examine its different but interrelated causal elements: population growth, economic growth, development of new technologies and modern management techniques. First, however, we need to consider briefly a fact which is often neglected in the present environmental discussions: namely, that industry and technology have always endangered the working conditions and health of the factory worker. The early socialists of the 19th century realised this as clearly as did Marx and Engels. The social implications – long hours of work, unemployment, bad housing, child labour, etc. – of industrial change in the 19th century were felt by millions. There was also extensive air and water pollution in the cities. The improvement of the quality of life is thus by no means a new objective for trade unions, but should be seen as an extension of the traditional tasks and aims of trade unionism. What has changed radically are the nature and proportions of the environmental disruption and the resulting deterioration of the human condition. On the other hand, the problems of his social environment which were the prime concern of the worker in the 19th century are still central objectives of trade union activity.

The question arises whether the battle to protect and improve the quality of our natural and social environment also needs to be fought by trade unions. To answer this, we must first understand how the present ecological crisis arose and what means are necessary to combat the deterioration of the environment.

Causes of the ecocrisis

In arriving at a diagnosis of the present environmental disruption the economist can easily be misled by a number of prevalent partial explanations. Until recently the problem was largely ignored, then denied and finally dismissed. Now it is frequently explained by the rapid growth of population, urbanisation, the 'affluent society'; or by technology in general. Especially popular today are mathematically formulated extrapolations to the effect that we simply cannot afford an exponential growth in affluence and technology. While these factors have contributed to environmental disruption, they offer no satisfactory explanation of the catastrophic increase in pollution.[2] Global data obscure the specific causal relationships that we are seeking. We need empirical studies of the environmental problem and more sophisticated statistical methods. The economist needs to have a clear picture of the causes and degree of the disruption of the ecological equilibrium which industrial activity, including the choice of technology and location in terms of market costs and returns, have brought about.

In order to understand the ecological impact of economic activity we must view both the economy and the environment as open systems that stand in reciprocal relationship to each other. Modern technology and production are capable of destroying ecological equilibria by the emission of waste products and toxic substances. The ecological systems, which have hardly been studied in the physical sciences and have been totally ignored by economists, are highly complex circulatory systems, held in an unstable equilibrium by a continous cycle of chemical reactions of various sorts. The quality of the human environment as well as productivity depends on the ecological equilibrium. If this equilibrium is threatened so are production and human existence.[3]

The present catastrophic deterioration of the environment is far greater than could be expected from the global rates of population and economic growth. Thus it must be seen primarily as the result of economic decisions and a system of entrepreneurial accountancy which have paid little or no attention to the destructive tendencies and negative effects of production on the ecological equilibrium. If the production factors, which have their origin in post-war and Cold War attitudes to science and technology, have led to increases in production and productivity, and are therefore regarded as 'successful' in terms of the market calculus, then it must also be seen that in the light of the destruction of ecological equilibria and the deterioration of the quality of human life they have been an ecological failure, which in some cases, such as in Japan and the United States, appears to have reached a state of ecological bankruptcy.

Hence, in order to understand the causal processes of environmental disruption we should concern ourselves with the radical transformation of technology and the way in which new processes are applied without taking account of their effect on the ecological system, rather than considering global rates of growth. For this we need both empirical and theoretical research, as well as differentiated statistical measurements that are not simply based on aggregates. The research must not be restricted to industry, but must include agricultural production as well. As a simple example: the average consumption of beer has risen only slightly in the past 10-20 years. Yet the production of disposable bottles has increased greatly over the same period (by 595% between 1950 and 1967). Thus the greater 'affluence' achieved with a more convenient 'packaging' of the article has been bought at the price of a deterioration of the environment, while the actual consumption of the article itself has been roughly constant. On top of this, the consumption of energy and use of toxic substances in the manufacture of the 'disposable' bottles has also increased.[4]

Moreover, the accelerated deterioration of the environment can largely be ascribed to the introduction of identifiable inputs and products which have been introduced without due consideration of the negative effect on the ecosystem. This procedure is in harmony with the application of a principle which until now has not been seriously questioned: the principle of the market economy, i.e. the minimisation of costs, or the maximisation of net profits, expressed in monetary terms. All important decisions in agriculture, industry and the public sector are taken in accordance with this principle. Thus, returnable bottles were replaced by disposable ones, cotton and wool by synthetic fibres, soap by detergents, wood and bricks by steel, aluminum, concrete and plastics. Motor cars and heavy lorries are replacing rail traffic, thus adding to pollution and causing traffic congestion. In addition the use of tetra-ethyl lead in the modern combustion engine has greatly increased the lead levels[5] in the atmosphere, while levels of nitrogen oxides has risen sevenfold.

In agriculture we have increased the yield per acre with the aid of fertilisers and insecticides,[6] although we now know that part of these substances cannot be assimilated by the soil and endanger the water supply. Since the social cost of pollution are shifted to third persons, and society at large, and since the use of chemicals is obviously profitable, they continue to be widely used.

In industry modern organisational techniques and the improved flow of information is used to apply the market calculus more effectively in decision-making. But since only market values are used, which offer no criteria for the evaluation of environmental factors, these procedures offer no way of   resolving the ecocrisis. On the contrary, the crisis points to the limitations of present economic theorising. It shows that the market economy offers no guarantees against the destruction of the environment, its attempts at evaluation of environmental factors in monetary terms are wholly inadequate. We are therefore forced to reconsider the premises of the concept of economic rationality.

Economics of environmental protection
Before discussing some aspects of effective environmental policies, I wish to comment on the problem of the relative distribution of social costs among different income groups. This should be of interest to the trade union movement, but, more generally, it also has a bearing upon the formulation of criteria for environmental politics. Social costs in the form of air and water pollution, noise, slums, etc., are shifted onto third persons, other production units and society at large. Here we are faced with relations that differ radically from those determined by the market. The latter are more or less voluntarily determined, while the relations between production, environment and the individual are highly involuntary, with negative effects that are often not fully understood by the individual, but which he cannot escape. What is happening takes place 'behind his back', without offering him a possibility of weighing advantages and disadvantages against each other. In short, environmental relations are highly one-sided relationships forced on the individual.

Whenever social costs are shifted onto the economically and politically weaker sections of society without compensation, a redistribution of the costs of production, hence of real income, is involved. During the first Industrial Revolution it was undoubtedly the industrial proletariat which carried the burden of social costs, in low wages, long hours, high accident rates, social insecurity, etc. The present environmental dangers threaten all sections of the population but in unequal measure. The higher and middle income groups are able to evade the worst impact of pollution, noise and traffic chaos by moving to suburbs in the green belt areas, or to smaller towns, or by the installation of air-conditioning, etc. The poorer sections and the ghetto population have no means of evading the unhealthy working and living conditions, and are more exposed to noise, traffic chaos and pollution, with far less possibilities for recreation. For example: the concentration of toxic substances such as carbon monoxide and sulphur oxides is ten times higher in cities than in the country. In the city centres of the United States, which are more heavily populated by blacks and other minority groups, these toxic levels are much higher than in the suburbs. Similarly the lead content in the blood of city dwellers (in Cincinnati, Los Angeles, Philadelphia) increased noticeably during 1962-69 and higher concentrations were found among inhabitants of the city centres than among suburbanites. It is estimated that there are over 400,000 cases with abnormal lead content in the blood in the U.S.A. alone. Lead poisoning in children in New York City in 1970 was found in 2649 cases by a survey based on a sample of 87,000 children.[7]

Discussions of, and attempts at, environmental protection and control lie within a fairly wide spectrum ranging from more or less verbal 'solutions' to far-reaching controls and prohibition of damaging factors of production, restructuring of technology, control of siting and spacing of industrial complexes. There are both 'minimalists' and 'maximalists'. The former attempt to answer the problem by general suggestions and indirect controls while the latter claim that it is already impossible and too late to save the situation by an effective environmental policy.

All attempts to protect the environment within the framework of a market economy must be considered to be in the first category. To these we may also count all attempts to pass off the ecocrisis as falling within the province of public relations departments.[8]

The maximalists include those who maintain that only a radical cutback in the rates of growth can stem the tide of ecological destruction; they base their analysis on exponential growth rates or are inclined to shift the responsibility for reduction in growth onto the underdeveloped countries with high population increases. Between these two extremes there lie a gamut of proposals,[9] such as the improvement of information available to the market, the assignment of monetary values to environmental factors, or the sale of rivers and areas of natural beauty to private firms who would then see to it that their private property rights are protected or compensated for increase of pollution and deterioration. Most of these attempts are based on an extension of the price system to environmental problems, as are proposals for financial incentives to effect protection of the environment. One step further go suggestions of taxation and effluent charges with the revenues set aside for the restoration of the damaged areas. These proposals reflect a desire to prevent at all costs the application of environmental policies making use of direct controls which may upset the market system. Their aim seems to be to handle the ecocrisis without policies which are believed not to be compatible to the market system.

The danger to the environment, however, demands the formulation of environmental goals for the improvement of the quality of human life. Such goals and their realisation are social aims, directed toward the satisfaction of collective needs. The market cannot be relied upon to satisfy these needs; on the contrary, as we have pointed out the market creates self-destructive tendencies, especially in the presence of the application of dangerous technical processes. The market does not offer an adequate evaluation of these collective needs and social goods; it neither defines the necessary social aims nor their relative importance or their order of priority relative to other social objectives and constraints. Its norms and aims are based upon private net profit – this is the given aim of private enterprise economies. Hence these aims are not under discussion; they are clear and given *a priori* and can be expressed in monetary units. In this sense they are not 'problematical'.

Environmental goals, that is, the maintenance of essential ecological equilibria, are not given, nor are they inherent to the market system – therefore they have to be defined and must be built into the economic system from outside, i.e. by society. The formulation of these aims and the determination of their relative importance as well as their practical implementation represent new tasks and new problems for economic theory and economic policies. Upon their solution depends the successful handling of the problems raised by the ecological crisis.

In the light of the above diagnosis of the causes of the deterioration of environment I consider the following steps in the development of a realistic programme of environmental politics and control as essential:

1. The systematic, quantitative determination of basic ecological relationships and their disruption by specific techniques applied in modern industrial production. The results of such a continuous process of ecological stocktaking should be expressed in the form of *environmental indicators*.
2. The formulation of environmental *norms* or standards as practical goals of a sociopolitical programme of environmental protection.
3. The conscious social direction of science and research towards the systematic development of less dangerous techniques which place a smaller burden on the environment than our present methods of production.
4. The development of effective political and economic controls realise these goals.
5. The replacement of current cost-benefit analyses by a more comprehensive assessment which is capable of measuring total costs and benefits to society as a whole.
6. The assessment of the total economic effects of measures of environmental control, on costs, employment productivity and the structure of production.
7. The incorporation of the politics of environmental control and improvement of the quality of life into the democratic process and democratic decision-making.

To discuss these seven steps separately:

1. In the first place a systematic quantitative study of ecological relationships must be achieved through regular observation and measurement of changes in atmospheric conditions, water supply etc. A formulation of environmental goals is possible only in the light of precise knowledge of the natural environment, its power of self-regulation and the limits of its tolerance levels. In this category we place observations of population densities and their trends, as well as of limits on the availability of basic resources, and precise knowledge of pollution resulting from specific technological processes and products. Before developing an effective process of ecological decision-making, we must be able to determine with some accuracy the level of pollution caused by specific inputs and outputs. Such pollution coefficients can be calculated only as averages, because of local differences. Commoner rightly asserts that we need an inventory of ecological effects for all branches of production and advocates the calculation of 'pollution price tags' for the most important products.
2. The second step would consist of the establishment of environmental norms, i.e. the determination of appropriate limits of maximum tolerance levels of concentration of contaminants, as well as minimum standards for the maintenance of human health and wellbeing. These are physical standards or limits beyond which any further disruption becomes a threat to man. They need not be fixed uniformly or permanently; on the contrary, they should be established on the basis of existing data and be changed in the light of new knowledge and experience. Furthermore, they will have to be adapted to existing means (including the level of technology). In short, environmental norms are minimum requirements and as such, require a social evaluation and need to be sanctioned in our political decision-making process.
3. A conscious social direction of scientific research toward environmental control goes far beyond the development of cleansing techniques, filtering installations,

etc. It must include the development of technologies and products which do not impair the environment, or at least do so to a lesser degree than present methods. This includes processes aimed at an efficient use of raw materials and sources of energy, both from the point of view of minimization of costs and the reduction of the volume of damaging waste products. Equally important is the systematic development of techniques based on the recycling of waste products.

Until now these problems have received very little attention. Private expenditures on techniques for the reduction of environmental disruption still run at a fraction of the total research expenditure and are only a small percentage of expenditure on advertising and public relations. In other words a much greater part of public funds must be channeled into this type of research. At present the total expenditure on the development of less disruptive technology is minimal when compared to the resources used on space research and armaments.

4. There is an urgent need for the effective application of direct and indirect controls in order to achieve environmental goals; some direct controls will have to be applied with a view to securing the immediate cessation of production of materials which are shown to endanger health and even life. This applies particularly to substances which may have genetic or cancer generating effects. In some cases this may necessitate the closure of existing production lines, as has already happened in Japan. Furthermore, direct controls of siting through licensing systems must be considered. Industry may be compelled to set aside a percentage of total profits for the development of new and environmentally less dangerous techniques, and these can be encouraged through incentives or through legislation.

5. Cost-benefit analysis will need to be made more comprehensive by the consideration of environmental factors such as the physical damage caused or expected in industrial processes. These are rarely expressible in monetary terms, but lend themselves to a socio-political evaluation – see also 6 and 7. In any case many attempts to express environmental costs in monetary terms either through direct calculation of the social cost or indirectly by calculation of the costs of controls or by using the individual's willingness to pay for environmental control, appear to be problematical. Environmental needs do not only represent public needs but constitute basic physical requirements for such things as clean air, water, health and tranquility, which cannot be articulated in market terms or monetary units. Any attempt to do so seems to me to be an inadmissible re-interpretation of these needs in monetary terms and an evasion of the problem of social decision-making. The individual's willingness to pay for the cost of satisfying these needs is distorted by the unequal distribution of income and the resulting unequal purchasing power of different sections of the population. There is thus a need for a socio-political evaluation of benefits and costs outside the framework of the market economy.

6. The evaluation of the cost and economic effects of environmental control can only partly be done in monetary terms.[10] Without neglecting the cost problem it

seems necessary to warn against a tendency of overestimating the total cost, and in particular the cost to some industries, expressed as a percentage of their total production. According to American estimates most polluting industries would face costs arising from environmental controls running at far less than 1% of their total production, and only for the main polluters (paper and metal processing and chemical industries) is the percentage above 1%. They seem to be roughly equivalent to the cost of a 5% wage increase. Of course different firms would have different increases of costs, and some would be unable to maintain production at present levels without price increases or subsidies. But these firms are now shifting the social cost of their production onto third parties, and thus would merely be compelled to bear the total cost of their production. Furthermore, smaller firms would often be harder hit than large companies. Hence there exists a real danger of a further concentration of industrial production. Problems of shifting additional costs through higher prices will differ from industry to industry and will depend on the specific structure of the market.

It seems much more important to consider the effect of controls on the level of employment, and the GNP. Here there seems no general and uniform answer. But it seems clear that rising costs may cause a decrease in production and give rise to unemployment, another social cost. On the other hand the manufacture of equipment to reduce environmental deterioration as well as the development of new technologies will provide additional sources of employment. Though this does not imply that, as is claimed, labour set free by new modes of production will automatically be re-employed. It does at least point to some compensating factors. The traditional composition of the total product will change but not necessarily its level. On the other hand the quality of life and of the environment would improve due to more effective controls. It is misleading to maintain that either the employer or the employee would be hardest hit by new environmental controls; it is as meaningless to say that the taxpayer or consumer are hardest hit. Problems of the incidence and distribution of costs can only be assessed in the light of a quantitative analysis, which takes into account the manner in which the additional financial funds are raised. In addition, what needs to be analysed is not only the costs and their distribution, but also the nature and quantity of the social benefits that accrue from the lessening of environmental disruption. To divert attention from these benefits or delay the introduction of practical measures on the ground of the uncertainty of their costs would be a totally one-sided approach.

7. The incorporation of the politics of environmental protection and improvement of the quality of life into the democratic process seems to me to be one of the most important aspects we have to face. Environmental policies involve in the first place the protection of collective goods as well as the satisfaction of elementary human needs, which are endangered by the application of modern technology and the destruction of ecological equilibria. To this effect the achievement of practical goals is a primary objective; the solution of technical

problems by the efficient use of existing means is subsequent to this. The formation of social decisions regarding environmental aims seems to me to be central to the problem. Environmental norms are social aims, which should be determined by the participation of all in the democratic process. These are new social tasks and require political decisions which demand a greater degree of public participation. So far large parts of the population, which are directly threatened by environmental disruption, have had no opportunity to participate in the formulation of economic policy.[11] In the formulation of environmental aims it becomes both possible and necessary to effect such participation through public discussion and a mobilisation of public opinion. The question of the 'risk' we are prepared to take regarding the health and survival of humanity, or what sacrifices and danger we are prepared to accept, is a question of public and political morality. It is true that the risk of the increase in cancer, or genetic dangers, inherent in exposure to radiation can only be estimated very approximately on the basis of scientific data, but the question whether we are prepared to assume such risks cannot be decided on a 'scientific' basis. In short, it is not a matter for experts, but a political and moral question, i.e. a matter of public judgment. The same is true of other environmental decisions. Furthermore, the judgment of individuals immediately concerned (consumers, residents, workers and citizens in general) is highly relevant in deciding whether they are prepared to tolerate a nuclear power station or pollution of water or air in their vicinity. Of course here again, as in all democratic decision-making processes, there is a lack of information, and the information itself may be 'polluted'. Hence it is absolutely essential that there should be maximum publicity in order to clarify both the causes and dangers of pollution. This does not only involve new tasks at all levels of education, but for citizens in general, and particularly for the trade union movement. These tasks lie in the mobilisation of public opinion and in the creation of an active consciousness of the need for environmental norms in the representation of public interest on all executive bodies of environmental control. As long as this representation is absent, there is danger that even the best control systems will be undermined by vested interests and 'experts'.

The deterioration of the environment calls for a radical change of our traditional notions of determining what is economically justified. It calls for a basic modification of economic calculation, it poses at various levels the question as to the need of establishing institutions and new methods of economic controls designed to safeguard the ecological balance and the quality of life. In this sense the crisis of the environment contains all the elements for a radical change of our prevailing forms of economic organisation. If we do not succeed in redirecting the development of science and technology and in shaping productive activities in a manner adapted to the maintenance of some ecological balance and the quality of life, it is likely that the disruption of the physical and social environment will reach critical proportions the full impact of which will surpass the implications of the First Industrial Revolution because it would put in question the very foundations of human life and survival. It is correct that man, just as other organisms, is able to adapt himself to a deteriorating environment but such an adaption requires longer periods of time than are at our disposal in view of the rapid development and change of modern technology. Moreover, man's capacity to adapt is limited quite apart from the fact that a life with gas masks, as envisaged by the Director of the Japanese Research Institute for Environmental Control for the inhabitants of Tokyo, would represent a dehumanization and alienation of man which transcends all traditional meanings of these terms.

Footnotes

1. Recently 50 Osaka students were overcome by nausea at a basketball match, after failing to hear an air pollution warning signal. According to the director of the Tokyo Environmental Research Institute it may be necessary for the inhabitants of Tokyo to wear gasmasks as protection against acute bronchial diseases within ten years. Traffic wardens, etc., already wear air filter devices. Peter Smith, Japan: Economic Dream Ecological Nightmare, *The Ecologist* 18; Dec. 1971 pp 17-18.

2. It is indeed possible that population and production growth has provided the last straw for exceeding the tolerance limits in ecological cycles whose maintenance is essential for the maintenance of all life, including human life. These relationships are considered by few economists.

3. These ecological processes which yield organic building materials necessary for the preservation of life and reproduction, are self-steering: they are circular processes established over millions of years, which man has disturbed to some extent in the past, but has never been, as now, in a position to destroy. Modern technology has created the impression of freeing man increasingly from his dependence on nature, and her limitations, but this has now been proved by the ecocrisis to be a fatal illusion. Barry Commoner, *The Closing Circle*, New York 1971, p.14.

4. Commoner and two colleagues at the Centre for the Biology of Natural Systems at Washington University have calculated the annual growth rate of hundreds of products during the last 25 years have introduced rankings. They show that the production (and use) of environmentally dangerous substances increases faster than that of essential goods. The latter do not increase much faster than the population, though there have been new goods and changes in quality To achieve this the production of synthetic fibres has increased by 5,980%, mercury by 3930%, plastics by 1960%, nitrogen fertilisers by 1000%, aluminum by 680%, pesticides by 390%. Ibid. p.143.

5. Commoner, *op cit.* p.169. Detailed studies show that 90% of all car journeys are over less than 10 miles.

6. In Illinois consumption of nitrogen increased from 10,000 tons in 1945 to 600,000 tons in 1966. Average yield of corn per acre increased from 50 bushel in 1945-48 to 70 bushel in 1958 using ca. 100,000 tons of nitrogen. In 1965 500,000 tons were needed to increase the average yield by another 20 bushel (to 90) per acre. That is to say in intense agriculture average yields per acre can be raised by disproportionate additional inputs of fertilisers. Ibid. p.84.

7. The incidence of lung cancer is 37% higher in cities of more than 1 million inhabitants than in cities housing 1/4 to 1 million. See Commoner *op cit.* pp. 134/5. See also *Environmental Quality*, Second Report, Washington, 1971, pp. 189-200 and Paul C. Craig and Edward Berlin, The air of poverty, *Environment*, 13, No.5, June 1971, pp.2-9.

8. The state of this 'environmental control' is reflected in a study (in which the 500 largest American firms were asked to name *one* project reflecting their social responsibility for environmental quality. 200 firms failed to reply, 100 could not mention any project, 100 named old and irrelevant projects, and only 50 had projects that answered the description, while the other 50 had borderline projects in hand. cf. Herbert Gross, *Beratungsbrief*, 39, Dusseldorf 1970 pp.4-5. An example of misleading advertising is the by now notorious photograph issued by a paper factory in the USA purporting to show a clean river downstream from the factory. In fact the picture showed the river 50 miles upstream! *Ibid* p.5.

9. An attempt at a comprehensive and detailed discussion of the methods of environmental control is given in K.W. Kapp, *Implementation of Environmental Policies*, in United Nations Development and Environment, Mouton, The Hague 1972.

10. OECD estimates show that the costs of environmental control would run at 5-6% of GNP in developed countries. Such estimates are still as problematic as estimates of social costs which are placed at 16 billion dollars spent on air pollution alone in the U.S.A. One must remember that these are very partial estimates. Global cost estimates have the disadvantage of omitting unit costs (e.g. per motor car mile, etc.) and give a misleading impression of prohibitive costs. Cf. M.H. Hyman, 'Timetable for Lead' *Environment*, 13, no.5, 1971, pp. 14-23.

11. cf. Jurgen Habermass, *Technik und Wissenschaft als ideologie*, Frankfurt 1969, pp.77-79. Habermass discusses the 'depoliticisation' of the general public and their elimination from the formulation of economic policies.

Meeting Social Needs

Mike Cooley

Mike Cooley was nominated for the Nobel Prize for his work with the Lucas Aerospace Shop Stewards on the development of socially useful products when the arms industry appeared to be scheduled for serious restructuring.

There are many contradictions which highlight the problems of our so-called technologically advanced society. Four of these contradictions are particularly relevant to what I shall have to say.

Firstly, there is the appalling gap which now exists between that which technology could provide for society and that which it actually does provide. We have a level of technological sophistication such that we can design and produce Concorde, yet in the same society we cannot provide enough simple heating systems to protect old age pensioners from hypothermia. In the winter of 1975-76, 980 died of the cold in the London area alone. We have senior automotive engineers who sit in front of computerised visual display units 'working interactively to optimize the configuration' of car bodies such that they are aerodynamically stable at 120 miles an hour when the average speed of traffic through New York is 6.2 miles an hour. It was in fact 11 miles per hour at the turn of the century when the vehicles were horse-drawn. In London at certain times of the day it is about 8.5 miles an hour. We have sophisticated communication systems such that we can send messages round the world in nano seconds, yet it now takes longer to send a letter from Washington to New York than it did in the days of the stagecoach. Hence we find the linear drive forward of complex esoteric technology in the interests of the multinational corporations and on the other hand the growing deprivation of communities and the mass of people as a whole.

The second contradiction is the tragic wastage our society makes of its most precious asset – that is the skill, ingenuity, energy, creativity and enthusiasm of its ordinary people. We now have in Britain 1.6 million people out of work. There are thousands of engineers suffering the degradation of the dole queue when we urgently need cheap, effective and safe transport systems for our cities. There are thousands of electricians robbed by society of the right to work when we urgently need economic urban heating systems. We have, I believe, 180,000 building workers out of a job when by the government's own statistics it is admitted that about 7 million people live in semi-slums in this country. In the London area we have about 20 per cent of the schools without an indoor toilet, when the people who could be making these things are rotting away in the dole queue.

The third contradiction is the myth that computerisation, automation and the use of robotic equipment will automatically free human beings from soul-destroying, back-breaking tasks and leave them free to engage in more creative work. The perception of my members and that of millions of workers in the industrial nations is that, in most instances, the reverse is actually the case.

Fourthly, there is the growing hostility of society at large to science and technology as at present practised. If you go to gatherings where there are artists, journalists and writers and you admit to being a technologist, they treat you as some latter day Yahoo, to misquote Swift. They really seem to believe that you specified that rust should be sprayed on car bodies before the paint is applied, that all commodities should be enclosed in non-recycleable containers, and that every large-scale plant you design is produced specifically to pollute the air and the rivers. There seems to be no understanding of the manner in which scientists and technologists are used as mere messenger boys of the multinational corporations whose sole concern is the maximisation of profits. It is therefore not surprising that some of our most able and sensitive sixth formers will now not study science and technology because they correctly perceive it to be such a dehumanised activity in our society.

All these four contradictions – and indeed many others – have impacted themselves upon us in Lucas Aerospace over the past five years. We do work on equipment for Concorde, we have experienced structural unemployment, and we know day by day of the growing hostility of the public to science and technology.

Lucas Aerospace was formed in the late 1960s when parts of the Lucas Industries took over sections of GEC, AEI and a number of other small companies. It was clear that the company would engage in a rationalisation programme along the lines already established by Arnold Weinstock in GEC. This, it will be recalled, was the time of Harold Wilson's 'white heat of technological change'. The taxpayer's money was being used through the Industrial Reorganisation Corporation to facilitate this rationalisation programme. No account at all was taken of the social cost: Arnold Weinstock subsequently sacked 60,000 highly skilled workers. This may have made GEC look efficient but the taxpayer had to pick up the tab, firstly for the payment of social services and, secondly, the nation state as a whole suffered the loss of the productive capacity of these talented workers.

We in Lucas Aerospace were fortunate in the sense that this happened about one year before our company embarked on its rationalisation programme. We were therefore able to build up a combined committee which would prevent the company setting one site against the other in the manner Weinstock had done. This body – the combined committee – is unique in the British trade union movement in that it links together the highest level technologists and the semi-skilled workers on the shop floor. There is therefore a creative cross-fertilisation between the analytical power of the scientist and the technologist on the one hand, and, perhaps what is much more important, the direct class sense and understanding of those on the shop floor. As structural unemployment began to affect us, we looked around at the manner in which other groups of workers were attempting to resist it. We had in Lucas already been engaged in partial sit-ins, in preventing the transfer of work from one site to another, and a host of other industrial tactics which had been developed over the past five years. But we realised that the morale of a workforce very quickly declines if they can see that society, for whatever reason, does not want the products that they make. *We therefore evolved the idea of a campaign for the right to work on socially useful products.*

The Lucas proposals

It seemed absurd to us that we had all this skill and knowledge and facilities and that society urgently needed equipment and services which we could provide, and yet the market economy seemed incapable of linking these two. What happened next provides an important object lesson for those who wish to analyse how society can be changed.

We prepared 180 letters which described in great detail the nature of the workforce, its skills, its age, its training, the machine tools, equipment and laboratories that were available to us and the types of scientific staff, together with the design capabilities which they had. We wrote to 180 leading authorities, institutions, universities, organisations and trade unions, all of which in the past had in one way or another suggested that there was a need for the humanisation of technology and the use of technology in a socially responsible fashion. What happened really was a revelation to us: all of these people who had made great speeches up and down the country, in some instances written voluminous books about these matters, were smitten into silence by the specificity of our request. We had asked them very directly what could a workforce with these facilities be making that would be in the interest of the community at large, and they were silent with the exception of four individuals: Dr Elliott at the Open University, Professor Thring at Queen Mary College, and Richard Fletcher and Clive Latimer at the North East London Polytechnic.

We then did what we should have done in the first instance: we asked our own members what they thought they should be making. I have never doubted the ability of ordinary people to cope with these problems, but not doubting it is one thing, having concrete evidence is something different. That concrete evidence began to pour into us within three or four weeks. In a short time we had 150 ideas of products which we could make and build with the existing machine tools and skills we had in Lucas Aerospace. We elicited this information through our shop stewards' committees via a questionnaire. I should explain that this questionnaire was very different from those which the soap powder companies produce where the respondent is treated as some kind of passive cretin. In our case, the questionnaire was dialectically designed. By that I mean that, in filling it in, the respondent was caused to think about his or her skill and ability, the environment in which he or she worked, and the facilities which they had available to them. We also deliberately composed it so that they would think of themselves in their dual role in society, that is both as producers and as consumers. We therefore quite deliberately transcended the absurd division which our society imposes on us, which seems to suggest that there are two nations, one that works in factories and offices, and an entirely different nation that lives in houses and communities. We pointed out that what we do during the day at work should be meaningful in relation to the communities in which we live. We also deliberately designed the questionnaire to cause the respondents to think of products not merely for their exchange value but for their use value.

When we collected all these proposals we refined them into six major product ranges which are now embodied in six volumes, each of approximately 200 pages. They contain specific technical details, economic calculations and even engineering drawings. We quite deliberately sought a mix of products which, on the one hand, included those which could be designed and built in the very short term, and those which would require long-term development; those which could be used in metropolitan Britain mixed with those which would be suitable for use in the Third World, products incidentally which could be sold in a mutually non-exploitative fashion. Finally, we sought a mix of products which would be profitable by the present criteria of the market economy and those which would not necessarily be profitable but would be highly socially useful.

Products for the community

I shall explain briefly some of the products we are proposing.

In the medical field Lucas already makes pacemakers and kidney machines. About three years ago, the company attempted to sell off its kidney machine division to an international company operating from Switzerland. We were able to prevent them doing so at that time both by threats of action and the involvement of some MPs. When we checked on the requirements for kidney machines in Britain we were horrified to learn that 3,000 people die each year because they cannot get a kidney machine. If you are under 25 and over 55 it is almost impossible in many areas to get one. The doctors involved sit like judge and juries with the governors of hospitals deciding who will be allowed, as they so nicely put it, 'to go into decline'. One doctor said to us how distressed he was by this situation and admitted that sometimes he did not tell the families of the patients that this was happening because they would otherwise be distressed. We regard it as outrageous that the skilled workers who design and make this equipment face the prospect of the dole queue where they will be paid about £40 a week (which when administered by the bureaucrats is approximately £70 a week), when with a little commonsense if they were paid £70 a week to stay in industry they could at least be producing artefacts which will be required by society. Indeed, if the social contract meant anything and if there were such a thing as a social wage, surely this is precisely the sort of thing which it should imply, namely, having foregone wage increases in order that we could expand the services to the community at large, we should have the opportunity of producing medical equipment which they require.

Before we even started the corporate plan, our members at the Wolverhampton plant visited a centre for children with Spina Bifida and were horrified to see that the only way they could propel themselves about was literally by crawling on the floor. So they designed a vehicle which subsequently became known as Hobcart – it was highly successful and the Spina Bifida Association of Australia wanted to order 2,000 of these. Lucas would not agree to manufacture these because they said it was incompatible with their product range and at that time the corporate plan was not developed and we were not able to press for this. But the design and development of this product were significant in another sense: Mike Parry Evans, its designer, said that it was one of the most enriching experiences of his life when he actually took the Hobcart down and saw the pleasure on the child's face – it meant more to him, he said, than all the design activity he had been involved in up to then. For the first time in his career *he actually saw the person who was going to use the product that he had designed.* It was enriching also in another sense because he was intimately in contact with a social human problem. He literally had to make a clay mould of the child's back so that the seat would support it properly. It was also fulfilling in that for the first time he was working in the multi-disciplinary team together with a medical type doctor, a physiotherapist and a health visitor. I mention this because it illustrates very graphically that it is untrue to suggest that aerospace technologists are only interested in complex esoteric technical problems. It can be far more enriching for them if they are allowed to relate their technology to really human and social problems.

Some of our members at another plant realised that a significant percentage of the people who die of heart attacks die between the point at which the attack occurs and the stage at which they are located in the intensive care unit in the hospital. So they designed a light, simple, portable life support system which can be taken in an ambulance or at the side of a stretcher to keep the patient 'ticking over' until they are linked to the main life support system in the hospital. They also learned that many patients die under critical operations because of the problem of maintaining the blood at a constant optimum temperature and flow. This, it seemed to them, was a simple technical problem if one were able to get behind the feudal mysticism of the medical profession. So they designed a fairly simple heat exchanger and pumping system and they built this in prototype. I understand that when the assistant chief designer at one of our plants had to have a critical operation, they were able to convince the local hospital to use it and it was highly successful.

In the field of alternative energy sources we have come up with a very imaginative range of proposals. It seemed to us absurd that it takes more energy to keep New York cool during the summer than it does to heat it during the winter.

If, therefore, there were systems which could conserve this energy at a time when it is not required and use it at a time when it is, this would make a lot of sense. One of the proposals for storing energy in this way was to produce gaseous hydrogen fuel cells. These would require considerable funding from the government but would produce means of conserving energy which would be ecologically desirable and socially responsible. We also designed a range of solar collecting equipment which could be used in low energy houses, and we worked in conjunction with Clive Latimer and his colleagues at the North East London Polytechnic in producing components for a low energy house. I should add that this house was specifically designed so that it could be constructed on a self-build basis. In fact, some of the students working on the Communications Design Degree course at that polytechnic are now writing an instruction manual which would enable people without any particular skills to go through a learning process and at the same time to produce very ecologically desirable forms of housing. One can now see that if this concept were linked to imaginative government community funding it would be possible in areas of high unemployment where there are acute housing problems to provide funds to employ those in that area to build their own housing.

We have made a number of contacts with county councils as we are very keen to see that these products are used in communities at large. We are unhappy about the present tendency of alternative technology for products to be provided which are little more than playthings for the middle class in their architect-built houses. Hence, we have already made links via the Open University with the Milton Keynes Corporation and have designed and are currently building in conjunction with the OU prototype heat pumps which will use natural gas and will increase the actual coefficient of performance (COP) by 2.8 times.

Drawing on our aerodynamics knowhow, we have proposed a range of wind generators. In some instances these would have a unique rotor control in which the liquid which is used as the media for transmitting the heat is actually used to achieve the breaking and is thereby heated in the process itself.

We have proposed a range of products which would be useful in Third World countries. We feel, incidentally, that we should be very humble about suggesting that our kind of technology would be appropriate in these countries; if one looks at the incredible mess we have made of technology in our society, probably one of the most important things the Third World countries could learn from us is what not to do rather than what to do! It is also a very arrogant assumption to believe that the only form of technology is that which we have in the West. I can see no reason why there should not be technologies which are compatible with the cultural and social structures of these other countries. At the moment, our trade with these countries is essentially neo-colonialist. We seek to introduce forms of technology which will make them dependent upon us. When the 'gin and tonic brigade' go out to sell a power pack, for example, they always seek to sell a dedicated power pack for each application, that is one power pack for generating electricity, another power pack for pumping water, and so on. We have proposed a unique power pack which could operate on a range of indigenous fuels and methane and which, by means of a variable speed gearbox, would be capable of alternatively pumping water, compressing air, providing high pressure hydraulics and generating electricity. This would, therefore, be a sort of universal power pack which could provide a small village or community with a range of services. This is quite contrary to the present design methodology which seeks to do the reverse.

Time and space does not permit a detailed account of the rest of the 150 products. Three further ones, however, are worth describing.

We are proposing a hybrid power pack which could be used in cars, coaches, lorries or trains. There is now a growth in the use of battery driven vehicles. This is clearly ecologically desirable but has the great disadvantage that in a stop-start situation they have to be charged every 40 miles, and on a flat terrain about every hundred miles. We are proposing a power pack in which we have a small internal combustion engine running at its constant optimum revs: this will mean that all the energy which is lost as one accelerates, decelerates, idles at traffic lights, starts cold and so on, is put in as useful energy through a generator which charges a stack of batteries which then operates an electric motor. Our initial calculations (which have subsequently been supported by work done in Germany) suggest that this would improve specific fuel consumption by 50 per cent; it would reduce toxic emissions, since the unburned gases are not going out into the atmosphere, to about 80 per cent. Further, since the whole system would be running at constant revs, one could calculate all the resonance of the system and effectively silence it: our calculations suggest that a power pack of this kind would be inaudible against a background noise of about 60 or 70 decibels at 10 metres.

It may be asked, of course, why such a power pack had not been designed and developed before. The simple answer, it seems to us, is that such a power pack would have to last for about ten or fifteen years, and this is absolutely contrary to the whole ethos of automotive design which has as its basis the notion of a throw-away product with all the terrible waste of energy and materials which that implies. We are convinced that Western society cannot carry on in this wasteful and arrogant fashion much longer.

This work has caused us to question very fundamentally the underlying assumptions of industries such as the automotive industry. We have had long discussions with our colleagues at Chryslers and British Leyland. In fact the workers at Chryslers now see that the choice facing them two or three years ago was not to continue producing rubbishy cars or to face the dole queue. There were a whole series of other options open to them if the political and social infrastructure were there to allow them to do so. We have been working with Richard Fletcher and his colleagues at the North East London Polytechnic on a unique road-rail vehicle which is capable or driving through a city as a coach and then running on the national railway network. It could provide the basis for a truly integrated, cheap, effective public transport system in this country. It uses pneumatic tyres and is therefore capable of going up an incline of 1:6 – normal railway rolling stock can only go up an incline of 1:80. This meant in the past that when a new railway line was laid down it was necessary literally to flatten the mountains and fill up the valleys or put tunnels through them. This costs about £1 million per track mile – this was the approximate cost of the railway in Tanzania which the Chinese put down. With our system a track can be put down at about £20,000 per track mile since it follows the natural contours of the countryside. This vehicle would therefore not only be of enormous use in metropolitan Britain but would also be of great interest in developing countries and even in areas such as Scotland and some of the less densely populated areas in Europe.

The last range of equipment I would like to mention is what we call telearchic devices. This literally means hands or control at a distance. If we examine the present development of technology, we will see that machines and systems are designed in such a fashion as to objectivise human skill and thereby diminish or totally replace the human being. This means in practice that industries are becoming capital intensive rather than labour intensive. These are also invariably energy intensive. This is now giving rise to massive structural unemployment in all of the technologically advanced nations. There have been about five million permanent unemployed in the United States over the past ten years; in Britain we have now got 1.6 million. Even in West Germany, that most optimistic of technologically advanced nations, they now have one million people out of work and 700,000 on short-time working. In 1974, they increased the number of process computers by 50.3 per cent and, in 1975, by 33.8 per cent. They will have 60 times as many microprocessors by 1984 and they reckon that, in 1982, 60 per cent of all measuring and control equipment will include these microprocessors. It is clear that this is going to give rise to a massive dislocation of the workforce and these concerns are now being expressed by the West German trade union movement, in particular by Ulrich Briefs of the DGB (German TUC). Gradually, they too are learning that the more we invest in industry in its present form, the more people we put out of work. When we were considering the design of robotic equipment to maintain North Sea oil piplines, the more we thought about this the more it became clear the terrible waste we are making of the great human intelligence which is available to us. If you try to design a robot to recognise which way a hexagon nut is about, much less to select the correct spanner to use on it and then to apply the correct torque, it is an incredible programming job and you realise how intelligent people are in the sense that they can do this without really 'even thinking about it'. In fact comparisons we have made show that the most complicated robotic equipment with pattern recognition intelligence has intelligence units of 103, whereas human beings have synaptic connections of 1014. There is therefore no comparison even at a theoretical level between the intelligence of human beings and the intelligence of these artificial devices. Yet with the linear drive forward of science and technology we deliberately design equipment to eliminate all that vast human knowledge.

So we are proposing these telearchic devices which reverse the historical tendency to diminish or objectivise human skill. Basically they are a range of equipment which will mimic in real time the motions of a human being. This would mean that in the case of mining, the skill of the miner would still be used but the miner could go through the mining process remotely in a safe environment whilst the telearchic device actually did the mining for him. Thus, we human beings would continue to be involved in that precious learning process, which comes about through actually working on the physical world about us, and it would also mean that we would be countering structural unemployment. We would, in a word, be very creatively linking a relatively labour-intensive form of work with a reasonably advanced and responsible technology. We would not therefore be proposing a return to the so-called 'good old days' in which some romantics seem to believe that the populace spent its time dancing round maypoles in unspoiled meadows. We are deeply conscious of the squalor, the disease, the filth which existed in the past and the contribution science and technology has made in overcoming these. What we believe is necessary is to draw on that which is best from our past and link it with that which is best in our science and technology.

Harnessing technology to human needs

The Lucas workers' corporate plan has the distinct advantage that it is a very concrete proposal put forward by a group of well organised industrial workers who have demonstrated in the past, by the products they have designed and built, that they are no daydreamers. It is proving to be a unique vehicle with which to test the boundaries of the system in a technological, political and economic sense.

We have of course approached the government and we have had every sympathy short of actual help. We have been enormously impressed at the ability of the various ministries to pass the buck; indeed, we have experienced at first hand the white heat of bureaucracy. Although the company has centrally rejected the corporate plan and is now refusing to meet the combined committee to discuss it, no Minister has been prepared to insist that the company should meet us to do so. In fact junior ministers, like Les Huckfield, continually write to us saying 'In my considered view those best suited to deal with this question are the company and the trade unions involved'. It is absolutely clear that the company will not and has not met us to discuss the plan. However, support from the trade union movement is growing – large shop stewards' committees at Chryslers, Vickers, Rolls Royce and elsewhere are now discussing corporate plans of this kind. One of our colleagues from Burnley, Terry Moran, has made a tour of trades councils in Scotland discussing these matters. The combined committee is now itself organising a series of meetings in the towns in which Lucas Aerospace has sites. We think it is arrogant for aerospace technologists to believe that they should be defining what communities should have. We are seeking through the local trade unions, political parties and other organisations in each area to help us to define what they need and to begin to create a climate of public opinion where we can force the government and the company to act. At the national level the TUC has produced a half an hour television programme on BBC2 dealing with our corporate plan: this is part of its TN training programme for shop stewards. The

Transport & General Workers Union has just come out with a statement indicating that its shop stewards throughout the country should press for corporate plans of this kind. At an international level the interest has been truly enormous. In Sweden, for example, they have produced six half-hour radio programmes dealing exclusively with the corporate plan and have made cassettes which are now being discussed in factories throughout Sweden. They have also made a half-hour television programme, and a paperback book has been produced dealing with the corporate plan. Similar developments are taking place in Australia and elsewhere and the interest centres not merely on the fact that a group of workers, for the first time, are demanding the right to work on socially useful products, but that they are proposing a whole series of new methods of production, where workers by hand and brain can really contribute to the design and development of products and where they can work in a non-alienated fashion in a labour process which enhances human beings rather than diminishes them.

Our society in the past has been very good at technical invention but very slow at social innovation. We have made incredible strides technologically but our social organisations are virtually those which existed several hundred years ago. One of the Swedish television interviews said 'when one looks at Britain in the past it has been great at *scientific and technological invention* and frequently has not really developed or exploited that. The Lucas workers corporate plan shows *great social invention* but it probably is also the case that they will not develop or extend that in Britain' (my italics). If this were true it would be very sad indeed.

The concluding point I would make is this. Science and technology are not given. It is not like the sun or the moon or the stars. It is man-made and if it does not do what we want then we have a right to change it. It is interesting to look at some of the adverts for tranquilisers: one I have here shows a woman dominated by what technology has done to her – high-rise flats, she is suffering from high-rise blues, and it says very subtly, 'she cannot change her environment but you can change her mood with Serenid D' – which incidentally is a tranquilliser. We in Lucas Aerospace are trying to say that it is not pills and tranquillisers we need but a very clear political and ideological view of what we want technology to do for us, and the courage and determination to fight for its implementation. We hope that in that fight we will be supported by widespread sections of the community because we will not be able to create an island of responsibility in Lucas Aerospace in a sea of depravity.

European Nuclear Disarmament

Ken Coates

This abridged article was published in Spokesman 38, *in 1980, and was later included in the collection* Eleventh Hour for Europe, *which appeared in 1981.*

'Remember your humanity, and forget the rest. If you can do so, the way lies open to a new Paradise; if you cannot, there lies before you the risk of universal death.'

Russell-Einstein Manifesto, 1955

The most dangerous decade in history ...

At the end of April 1980, following some months of consultation and preparation, an appeal for European Nuclear Disarmament was launched at a press conference in the House of Commons, and at meetings in a variety of European capital cities. The text of the appeal reads:

We are entering the most dangerous decade in human history. A third world war is not merely possible, but increasingly likely. Economic and social difficulties in advanced industrial countries, crisis, militarism and war in the Third World compound the political tensions that fuel a demented arms race. In Europe, the main geographical stage for the East-West confrontation, new generations of ever more deadly nuclear weapons are appearing.

For at least twenty-five years, the forces of both the North Atlantic and the Warsaw alliances have each had sufficient nuclear weapons to annihilate their opponents, and at the same time to endanger the very basis of civilised life. But with each passing year, competition in nuclear armaments has multiplied their numbers, increasing the probability of some devastating accident or miscalculation.

As each side tries to prove its readiness to use nuclear weapons, in order to prevent their use by the other side, new more 'usable' nuclear weapons are designed and the idea of 'limited' nuclear war is made to sound more and more plausible. So much so that this paradoxical process can logically only lead to the actual use of nuclear weapons.

Neither of the major powers is now in any moral position to influence smaller countries to forgo the acquisition of nuclear armament. The increasing spread of nuclear reactors and the growth of the industry that installs them, reinforce the likelihood of world-wide proliferation of nuclear weapons, thereby multiplying the risks of nuclear exchanges.

Over the years, public opinion has pressed for nuclear disarmament and détente between the contending military blocs. This pressure has failed. An increasing proportion of world resources is expended on weapons, even though mutual extermination is already amply guaranteed. This economic burden, in both East and West, contributes to growing social and political strain, setting in motion a vicious circle in which the arms race feeds upon the instability of the world economy and vice versa: a deathly dialectic.

We are now in great danger. Generations have been born beneath the shadow of nuclear war, and have become habituated to the threat. Concern has given way to apathy. Meanwhile, in a world living always under menace, fear extends through both halves of the European continent. The powers of the military and of internal security forces are enlarged, limitations are placed upon free exchanges of ideas and between persons, and civil rights of independent-minded individuals are threatened, in the West as well as the East.

We do not wish to apportion guilt between the political and military leaders of East and West. Guilt lies squarely upon both parties. Both parties have adopted menacing postures and committed aggressive actions in different parts of the world.

The remedy lies in our own hands. We must act together to free the entire territory of Europe, from Poland to Portugal, from nuclear weapons, air and submarine bases, and from all institutions engaged in research into or manufacture of nuclear weapons. We ask the two superpowers to withdraw all nuclear weapons from European territory. In particular, we ask the Soviet Union to halt production of the SS-20 medium range missile and we ask the United States not to implement the decision to develop cruise missiles and Pershing II missiles for deployment in Europe. We also urge the ratification of the SALT II agreement, as a necessary step towards the renewal of effective negotiations on general and complete disarmament.

At the same time, we must defend and extend the right of all citizens, East or West, to take part in this common movement and to engage in every kind of exchange.

We appeal to our friends in Europe, of every faith and persuasion, to consider urgently the ways in which we can work together for these common objectives. We envisage a European-wide campaign, in which every kind of exchange takes place; in which representatives of different nations and opinions confer and co-ordinate their activities; and in which less formal exchanges, between universities, churches, women's organisations, trade unions, youth organisations, professional groups and individuals, take place with the object of promoting a common object: to free all of Europe from nuclear weapons.

We must commence to act as if a united, neutral and pacific Europe already exists. We must learn to be loyal, not to 'East' or 'West', but to each other, and we must disregard the prohibitions and limitations imposed by any national state.

It will be the responsibility of the people of each nation to agitate for the expulsion of nuclear weapons and bases from European soil and territorial waters, and to decide upon its own means and strategy, concerning its own territory. These will differ from one country to another, and we do not suggest that any single strategy should be imposed. But this must be part of a continental movement in which every kind of exchange takes place.

We must resist any attempt by the statesmen of East and West to manipulate this movement to their own advantage. We offer no advantage to either Nato or the Warsaw alliance. Our objectives must be to free Europe from confrontation, to enforce détente between the United States and the Soviet Union, and, ultimately, to dissolve both great power alliances.

In appealing to fellow Europeans, we are not turning our backs on the world. In working for the peace of Europe we are working for the peace of the world. Twice in this century Europe has disgraced its claims to civilisation by engendering world war. This time we must repay our debts to the world by engendering peace.

This appeal will achieve nothing if it is not supported by determined and inventive action, to win more people to support it. We need to mount an irresistible pressure for a Europe free of nuclear weapons.

We do not wish to impose any uniformity on the movement nor to pre-empt the consultations and decisions of those many organisations already exercising their influence for disarmament and peace. But the situation is urgent. The dangers steadily advance. We invite your support for this common objective, and we shall welcome both your help and advice.

Several hundred people, many of whom were prominent in their own field of work, had already endorsed this statement before its publication. They included over sixty British MPs from four different political parties, and a number of peers, bishops, artists, composers and university teachers. The press conference, which was addressed by Tony Benn, Eric Heffer, Mary Kaldor, Bruce Kent, Zhores Medvedev, Dan Smith and Edward Thompson, launched a campaign for signatures to the appeal and by Hiroshima Day (August 6th, the anniversary of the dropping of the first atomic bomb on Japan) influential support had been registered in many different countries. Writers such as Kurt Vonnegut, Olivia Manning, John Berger, Trevor Griffiths, J.B. Priestley and Melvyn Bragg had joined with church leaders, political spokesmen, painters (Joan Miro, Vasarely, Josef Herman, David Tindle, Piero Dorazio), Nobel Prize winners and thousands of men and women working in industry and the professions. British signatories included the composer Peter Maxwell Davies, the doyen of cricket commentators, John Arlott, distinguished soldiers such as Sir John Glubb and Brigadier M.N. Harbottle, and trade union leaders (Moss Evans, Laurence Daly, Arthur Scargill and many others). It was generally agreed that a European meeting was necessary, in order to work out means of developing the agitation, and in order to discuss all the various issues and problems which are in need of elaboration, over and beyond the text of the appeal.

The Bertrand Russell Foundation is working on the preparation of this Conference. A small liaison committee has been established to coordinate the work in Great Britain, and various persons and groups have accepted the responsibility for co-ordinating action in particular fields of work. For instance, a group of parliamentarians will be appealing to their British colleagues, but also to MPs throughout Europe; academics will be writing to their own immediate circles, but also seeking international contacts; churches are being approached through Pax Christi; and an active trade union group has begun to develop.

'A demented arms race ...'

1980 began with an urgent and concerned discussion about rearmament. The Pope, in his New Year Message, caught the predominant mood: 'What can one say', he asked, 'in the face of the gigantic and threatening military arsenals which especially at the close of 1979 have caught the attention of the world and especially of Europe, both East and West?'

War in Afghanistan; American hostages in Tehran, and dramatic pile-ups in the Iranian deserts, as European-based American commandos failed to 'spring' them; wars or threats of war in South East Asia, the Middle East, and Southern Africa: at first sight, all the world in turbulence, excepting only Europe. Yet in spite of itself Europe is at the fixed centre of the arms race; and it is in Europe that many of the most fearsome weapons are deployed. What the Pope was recognising at the opening of the decade was that conflicts in any other zone might easily spill back into the European theatre, where they would then destroy our continent.

Numbers of statesmen have warned about this furious accumulation of weapons during the late 'seventies. It has been a persistent theme of such eminent neutral spokesmen as Olof Palme of Sweden, or President Tito of Yugoslavia. Lord Mountbatten, in his last speech, warned that 'the frightening facts about the arms race ... show that we are rushing headlong towards a precipice'.[1] Why has this 'headlong rush' broken out? First, because of the world-wide division between what is nowadays called 'North' and 'South'. In spite of United Nations initiatives, proposals for a new economic order which could assist economic development have not only not been implemented, but have been stalemated while conditions have even been aggravated by the oil crisis. Poverty was never morally acceptable, but it is no longer politically tolerable in a world which can speak to itself through transistors, while over and again in many areas starvation recurs. In others, millions remain on the verge of the merest subsistence. The Third World is thus a zone of revolts, revolutions, interventions, and wars.

To avoid or win these, repressive leaders like the former Shah of Iran are willing to spend unheard of wealth on arms, and the arms trade paradoxically often takes the lead over all other exchanges, even in countries where malnutrition is endemic. At the same time, strategic considerations bring into play the superpowers, as 'revolutionary' or 'counter-revolutionary' supports. This produces some extraordinary alignments and confrontations, such as those between the Ethiopian military and Somalia and Eritrea, where direct Cuban and Soviet intervention has been a crucial factor, even though the Eritreans have been engaged in one of the longest-running liberation struggles in all Africa: or such as the renewed Indo-China war following the Vietnamese invasion of Cambodia, in which remnants of the former Cambodian communist government appear to have received support from the United States, even though it only came into existence in opposition to American secret bombing, which destroyed the physical livelihood of the country together with its social fabric. A variety of such direct and indirect interventions owes everything to geopolitical expediency, and nothing to the ideals invoked to justify them. Such processes help promote what specialists call the 'horizontal' proliferation of nuclear weapons, to new, formerly non-nuclear states, at the same time that they add their pressure to the 'vertical' proliferation between the superpowers.

Second, the emergence of China into the community of nations (if this phrase can nowadays be used without cynicism) complicates the old pattern of interplay between the blocs. Where yesterday there was a tug o' war between the USA and the USSR, with each principal mobilising its own team of supporters at its end of the rope, now there is a triangular contest, in which both of the old-established contestants may, in future, seek to play the China team. At the moment, the Chinese are most worried about the Russians, which means that the Russians will feel a constant need to augment their military readiness on their 'second' front, while the Americans will seek to match Soviet preparedness overall, making no differentiation between the 'theatres' against which the Russians see a need for defence. It should be noted that the Chinese Government still considers that war is 'inevitable', although it has apparently changed its assessment of the source of the threat. (It is the more interesting, in this context, that the Chinese military budget for 1980 is the only one which is being substantially reduced, by $1.9 billion, or 8.5%).

Third, while all these political cauldrons boil, the military-technical processes have their own logic, which is fearsome.

Stacked around the world at the beginning of the decade, there was a minimum of 50,000 nuclear warheads belonging to the two main powers, whose combined explosive capacity exceeds by one million times the destructive power of the first atomic bomb which was dropped on Hiroshima. The number grows continually. This is 'global overkill'. Yet during the next decade, the USA and USSR will be manufacturing a further 20,000 warheads, some of unimaginable force ...

Limited war: the end of Europe?

In spite of détente, and the relatively stable relations between its two main halves during the past decade, Europe remains by far the most militaristic zone of the contemporary world.

At least 10,000, possibly 15,000, warheads are stockpiled in Europe for what is called 'tactical' or 'theatre' use. The Americans have installed something between 7,000 and 10,000 of these, and the Russians between 3,500 and 5,000. The yields of these weapons range, it is believed, between something less than one kiloton and up to three megatons. In terms of Hiroshima bombs, one three-megaton warhead would have the force of 250 such weapons. But nowadays this is seen as a 'theatre' armament, usable in a 'limited' nuclear war. 'Strategic' bombs, for use in the final stages of escalation, may be as large as 20 megatons. (Although, of course, those destined for certain types of targets are a lot smaller. The smallest could be a 'mere' 30 or 40 kilotons, or two or three Hiroshimas). Towns in Europe are not commonly far apart from one another. There exist no vast unpopulated tracts, plains, prairies or tundras, in which to confine a nuclear war. Military installations nestle among and between busy urban centres. As Zuckerman has insisted 'the distances between villages are no greater than the radius of effect of low yield weapons of a few kilotons; between towns and cities, say a megaton' ...

President Nixon first propounded the doctrine of limited nuclear war in his *State of the World* message of 1971. The USA, he said, needed to provide itself with 'alternatives appropriate to the nature and level of the provocation ... without necessarily having to resort to mass destruction'. Mountbatten, of course, is quite right to find it all incredible. 'I have never been able to accept the reasons for the belief that any class of nuclear weapons can be categorised in terms of their tactical or strategic purposes', he said.

As Lord Zuckerman put it to the Pugwash Conference:

'I do not believe that nuclear weapons could be used in what is now fashionably called a "theatre war"'. I do not believe that any scenario exists which suggests that nuclear weapons could be used in field warfare between two nuclear states without escalation resulting. I know of several such exercises. They all lead to the opposite conclusion. There is no Marquess of Queensberry who would be holding the ring in a nuclear conflict. I cannot see teams of physicists attached to military staffs who would run to the scene of a nuclear explosion and then back to tell their local commanders that the radiation intensity of a nuclear strike by the other side was such and such, and that therefore the riposte should be only a weapon of equivalent yield. If the zone of lethal or wounding neutron radiation of a so-called neutron bomb would have, say, a radius of half a kilometre, the reply might well be a "dirty" bomb with the same zone of radiation, but with a much wider area of devastation due to the blast and fire.'[2]

Pressure from the Allies has meant that Presidential statements on the issue of limited war have swung backwards and forwards. At times President Carter has given the impression that he is opposed to the doctrine. But the revelation of 'directive 59', in August 1980, shows that there is, in fact, a continuous evolution in US military policy, apparently regardless of political hesitations by Governments. Directive 59 is a flat-out regression to the pure Nixon doctrine. As the *New York Times* put it:

'(Defense Secretary) Brown seems to expand the very meaning of deterrence alarmingly. Typically, advocates of flexible targeting argue that it will deter a sneak attack. But Brown's speech says the new policy is also intended to deter a variety of lesser aggressions, ... including conventional military aggression ...'

Obviously, as the *NYT* claims, this is liable to increase the likelihood that nuclear weapons will be used'.[3]

Where would such weapons be used? That place would experience total annihilation, and in oblivion would be unable to consider the nicety of 'tactical' or 'strategic' destruction. If 'limited' nuclear exchanges mean anything at all, the only limitation which is thinkable is their restriction to a particular zone. And that is precisely why politicians in the United States find 'limited' war more tolerable than the other sort, because it leaves a hope that escalation to the total destruction of both superpowers might be a second-stage option, to be deferred during the negotiations which could be undertaken while Europe burns. It does not matter whether the strategists are right in their assumptions or not. There are strong reasons why a Russian counter-attack ought (within the lights of the Soviet authorities) to be directed at the USA as well as Europe, if Soviet military strategists are as thoughtful as we may presume. But the very fact that Nato is being programmed to follow this line of action means that Europeans must awaken to understand what a sinister mutation has taken place, beneath the continuing official chatter about 'deterrence'.

The fact that current Soviet military planning speaks a different language does not in the least imply that Europe can escape this dilemma. If one side prepares for a 'theatre' war in our continent, the other will, if and when necessary, respond, whether or not it accepts the protocol which is proposed for the orderly escalation of annihilation from superpower peripheries to superpower centres. The material reality which will control events is the scope and range of the weapons deployed: and the very existence of tens of thousands of theatre weapons implies, in the event of war, that there will be a 'theatre war'. There may be a 'strategic' war as well, in spite of all plans to the contrary. It will be too late for Europe to know or care.

All those missiles and bombs could never be used in Europe without causing death and destruction on a scale hitherto unprecedented and inconceivable. The continent would become a hecatomb, and in it would be buried, not only tens, hundreds of millions of people, but also the remains of a civilisation. If some Europeans survived, in Swiss shelters or British Government bunkers, they would emerge to a cannibal universe in which every humane instinct had been cauterised. Like the tragedy of Cambodia, only on a scale greatly wider and more profound, the tragedy of post-nuclear Europe would be lived by a mutilated people, prone to the most restrictive and destructive xenophobia, ganging for support into pathetic strong-arm squads in order to club a survival for themselves out of the skulls of others, and fearful of their own shadows. The worlds which came into being in the Florentine renaissance would have been totally annulled, and not only the monuments would be radioactive. On such deathly foundations, 'communism' may be installed, in the Cambodian manner, or some other more primary anarchies or brutalisms may maintain a hegemony of sorts. What is plain is that any and all survivors of a European theatre war will look upon the days before the holocaust as a golden age, and hope will have become, quite literally, a thing of the past.

A move towards European Nuclear Disarmament may not avoid this fearful outcome. Until general nuclear disarmament has been agreed and implemented no man or woman will be able to feel safe. But such a move may break the logic of the arms race, transform the meanings of the blocs, and begin a unified and irresistible pressure on both the superpowers to reverse their engines away from war.

We must act together …

If the powers want to have a bit of a nuclear war, they will want to have it away from home. And if we do not wish to be their hosts for such a match, then, regardless of whether they are right or wrong in supposing that they can confine it to our 'theatre', we must discover a new initiative which can move us towards disarmament. New technologies will not do this, and nor will introspection and conscience suddenly seize command in both superpowers at once.

We are looking for a *political* step which can open up new forms of public pressure, and bring into the field of force new moral resources, Partly this is a matter of ending superpower domination of the most important negotiations.

But another part of the response must involve a multinational mobilisation of public opinion. In Europe, this will not begin until people appreciate the exceptional vulnerability of their continent. One prominent statesman who has understood, and drawn attention to, this extreme exposure, is Olof Palme. During an important speech at a Helsinki Conference of the Socialist International, he issued a strong warning. 'Europe', he said, 'is no special zone where peace can be taken for granted. In actual fact, it is at the centre of the arms race. Granted, the general assumption seems to be that any potential military conflict between the superpowers is going to start someplace other than in Europe. But even if that were to be the case, we would have to count on one or the other party – in an effort to gain supremacy — trying to open a front on our continent, as well. As Alva Myrdal has recently pointed out, a war can simply be transported here, even though actual causes for war do not exist. Here there is a ready theatre war. Here there have been great military forces for a long time. Here there are programmed weapons all ready for action …'[4]

Basing himself on this recognition, Mr Palme recalled various earlier attempts to create, in North and Central Europe, nuclear-free zones, from which, by agreement, all warheads were to be excluded. (We look at the history of these proposals, below). He then drew a conclusion of historic significance, which provides the most real, and most hopeful, possibility of generating a truly continental opposition to this continuing arms race:

> 'Today more than ever there is, in my opinion, every reason to go on working for a nuclear-free zone. *The ultimate objective of these efforts should be a nuclear-free Europe.* (My emphasis.) The geographical area closest at hand would naturally be Northern and Central Europe. If these areas could be freed from the nuclear weapons stationed there today, the risk of total annihilation in case of a military conflict would be reduced.'

Olof Palme's initiative was launched exactly a month before the United Nations Special Session on Disarmament, which gave rise to a Final Document which is a strong, if tacit, indictment of the arms race that has actually accelerated sharply since it was agreed. A World Disarmament Campaign was launched in 1980, by Lord Noel Baker and Lord Brockway, and a comprehensive cross-section of voluntary peace organisations: it had the precise intention of securing the implementation of this Document. But, although the goal of the UN Special Session was 'general and complete disarmament' as it should have been, it is commonly not understood that this goal was deliberately coupled with a whole series of intermediate objectives, including Palme's own proposals. Article 33 of the statement reads:

> 'The establishment of nuclear-weapon-free zones on the basis of agreements or arrangements freely arrived at among the States of the zone concerned, and the full compliance with those agreements or arrangements, thus ensuring that the zones are genuinely free from nuclear weapons, and respect for such zones by nuclear-weapons States, constitute an important disarmament measure.'

Later, the declaration goes on to spell out this commitment in considerable detail. It begins with a repetition:

'The establishment of nuclear-weapons-free zones on the basis of arrangements freely arrived at among the States of the region concerned, constitutes an important disarmament measure,'

and then continues:

'The process of establishing such zones in different parts of the world should be encouraged with the ultimate objective of achieving a world entirely free of nuclear weapons. In the process of establishing such zones, the characteristics of each region should be taken into account. The States participating in such zones should undertake to comply fully with all the objectives, purposes and principles of the agreements or arrangements establishing the zones, thus ensuring that they are genuinely free from nuclear weapons.

With respect to such zones, the nuclear-weapon States in turn are called upon to give undertakings, the modalities of which are to be negotiated with the competent authority of each zone, in particular:

(a) to respect strictly the status of the nuclear-free zone;

(b) to refrain from the use or threat of use of nuclear weapons against the States of the zone …

States of the region should solemnly declare that they will refrain on a reciprocal basis from producing, acquiring, or in any other way, possessing nuclear explosive devices, and from permitting the stationing of nuclear weapons on their territory by any third party and agree to place all their nuclear activities under International Atomic Energy Agency safeguards.'

Article 63 of this final document schedules several areas for consideration as nuclear-free zones. They include Africa, where the Organisation of African Unity has resolved upon 'the denuclearisation of the region', but also the Middle East and South Asia, which are listed alongside South and Central America, whose pioneering treaty offers a possible model for others to follow. This is the only populous area to have been covered by an existing agreement, which was concluded by the Treaty of Tlatelolco (a suburb of Mexico City), opened for signature from February 1967.

There are other zones which are covered by more or less similar agreements. Conservationists will be pleased that they include Antarctica, the moon, outer space, and the seabed. Two snags exist in this respect. One is that the effectiveness of the agreed arrangements is often questioned. The other is that if civilisation is destroyed, the survivors may not be equipped to establish themselves comfortably in safe havens among penguins or deep-sea plants and fish, leave alone upon the moon.

That is why a Martian might be surprised by the omission of Europe from the queue of continents (Africa, Near Asia, the Far East all in course of pressing; and Latin America, with the exception of Cuba, already having agreed) to negotiate coverage within nuclear-free zones. If Europe is the most vulnerable region, the prime risk, with a dense concentration of population, the most developed and destructible material heritage to lose, and yet no obvious immediate reasons to go to war, why is there any hesitation at all about making Olof Palme's 'ultimate objective' into an immediate and urgent demand?

If we are agreed that 'it does not matter where the bombs come from', there is another question which is more pertinent. This is, where will they be sent to? Clearly, high priority targets are all locations from which response might otherwise come. There is therefore a very strong advantage for all Europe if 'East' and 'West', in terms of the deployment of nuclear arsenals, can literally and rigorously become coterminous with 'USA' and 'USSR'. This would constitute a significant pressure on the superpowers since each would thenceforward have a priority need to target on the silos of the other, and the present logic of 'theatre' thinking would all be reversed.

Nuclear-free zones in Europe

If Europe as a whole has not hitherto raised the issue of its possible denuclearisation, there have been a number of efforts to sanitise smaller regions within the continent.

The idea that groups of nations in particular areas might agree to forgo the manufacture or deployment of nuclear weapons, and to eschew research into their production, was first seriously mooted in the second half of the 1950s. In 1956, the USSR attempted to open discussions on the possible restriction of armaments, under inspection, and the prohibition of nuclear weapons, within both German States and some adjacent countries. The proposal was discussed in the Disarmament Sub-Committee of the United Nations, but it got no further. But afterwards the foreign secretary of Poland, Adam Rapacki, took to the Twelfth Session of the UN General Assembly a plan to outlaw both the manufacture and the harbouring of nuclear arsenals in all the territories of Poland, Czechoslovakia, the German Democratic Republic and the Federal German Republic. The Czechoslovaks and East Germans quicky endorsed this suggestion.

Rapacki's proposals would have come into force by four separate unilateral decisions of each relevant government. Enforcement would have been supervised by a commission drawn from Nato countries, Warsaw Pact adherents, and non-aligned states. Inspection posts, with a system of ground and air controls, were to be established to enable the commission to function. Subject to this supervision, neither nuclear weapons, nor installations capable of harbouring or servicing them, nor missile systems, would have been permitted in the entire designated area. Nuclear powers were thereupon expected to agree not to use nuclear weapons against the denuclearised zone, and not to deploy their own atomic warheads with any of their conventional forces stationed within it.

The plan was rejected by the Nato powers, on the grounds, first, that it did nothing to secure German reunification, and second, that it failed to cover the deployment of conventional armaments. In 1958, therefore, Rapacki returned with modified proposals. Now he suggested a phased approach. In the beginning, nuclear stockpiles would be frozen at their existing levels within the zone. Later, the removal of these weapon stocks would be accompanied by controlled and mutually agreed reductions in conventional forces. This initiative, too, was rejected.

Meanwhile, in 1957, Romania proposed a similar project to denuclearise the Balkans. This plan was reiterated in 1968, and again in 1972.

In 1959, the Irish Government outlined a plan for the creation of nuclear-free zones throughout the entire planet, which were to be developed region-by-region. In the same year, the Chinese People's Republic suggested that the Pacific Ocean and all Asia be constituted a nuclear-free-zone, and, in 1960, various African states elaborated similar proposals for an all-African agreement. (These were tabled again in 1965, and yet again in 1974).

In 1962, the Polish government offered yet another variation on the Rapacki Plan, which would have maintained its later notion of phasing, but which would now have permitted other European nations to join in if they wished to extend the original designated area. In the first stage, existing levels of nuclear weaponry and rocketry would be frozen, prohibiting the creation of new bases. Then, as in the earlier version, nuclear and conventional armaments would be progressively reduced according to a negotiated timetable. The rejection of this 1962 version was the end of the Rapacki proposals, but they were followed, in 1964, by the so-called 'Gomulka' plan, which was designed to affect the same area, but which offered more restricted goals.

Although the main Nato powers displayed no real interest in all these efforts, they did arouse some real concern and sympathy in Scandinavia. As early as October 1961, the Swedish government tabled what became known as the Undén Plan (named after Sweden's foreign minister) at the First Committee of the UN General Assembly. This supported the idea of nuclear-free zones and a 'non-atomic club', and advocated their general acceptance. Certain of its proposals, concerning non-proliferation and testing, were adopted by the General Assembly.

But the Undén Plan was never realised, because the USA and others maintained at the time that nuclear-free zones were an inappropriate approach to disarmament, which could only be agreed in a comprehensive 'general and complete' decision. Over and again this most desirable end has been invoked to block any less total approach to discovering any practicable means by which it might be achieved.

In 1963, President Kekkonen of Finland called for the reopening of talks on the Undén Plan. Finland and Sweden were both neutral already, he said, while Denmark and Norway, notwithstanding their membership of Nato, had no nuclear weapons of their own, and deployed none of those belonging to their Alliance. But although this constituted a *de facto* commitment, it would, he held, be notably reinforced by a deliberate collective decision to confirm it as an enduring joint policy.

The Norwegian premier responded to this *démarche* by calling for the inclusion of sections of the USSR in the suggested area. As long ago as 1959, Nikita Khrushchev had suggested a Nordic nuclear-free zone, but no approach was apparently made to him during 1963 to discover whether the USSR would be willing to underpin such a project with any concession to the Norwegian viewpoint. However, while this argument was unfolding, again in 1963, Khrushchev launched yet another similar proposal, for a nuclear-free Mediterranean.

The fall of Khrushchev took much of the steam out of such diplomatic forays, even though new proposals continued to emerge at intervals. In May 1974, the Indian government detonated what it described as a 'peaceful' nuclear explosion. This provoked renewed proposals for a nuclear-free zone in the Near East, from both Iran and the United Arab Republic, and it revived African concern with the problem. Probably the reverberations of the Indian bang were heard in New Zealand, because that nation offered up a suggestion for a South Pacific free-zone, later in the same year.

Yet, while the European disarmament lobbies were stalemated, the Latin American Treaty had already been concluded in 1967, and within a decade it had secured the adherence of 25 states. The last of the main nuclear powers to endorse it was the USSR, which confirmed its general support in 1978. (Cuba withheld endorsement because it reserved its rights pending the evacuation of the Guantanamo base by the United States.) African pressures for similar agreement are notably influenced by the threat of a South African nuclear military capacity, which is an obvious menace to neighbouring Mozambique, Zimbabwe, and Angola, and a standing threat to the Organisation of African Unity. In the Middle East, Israel plays a similar catalysing role, and fear of an Israeli bomb is widespread throughout the region.

Why, then, this lag between Europe and the other continents? If the pressure for denuclearised zones began in Europe, and if the need for them, as we have seen, remains direct there, why have the peoples of the Third World been, up to now, so much more effectively vocal on this issue than those of the European continent? Part of the answer surely lies in the prevalence of the Non-Aligned Movement among the countries of the Third World. Apart from a thin scatter of neutrals, Europe is the seed-bed of alignments, and the interests of the blocs as apparently disembodied entities are commonly prayed as absolute within it. In reality, of course, the blocs are not 'disembodied'. Within them, in military terms, superpowers rule. They control the disposition and development of the two major 'deterrents'. They keep the keys and determine if and when to fire. They displace the constituent patriotisms of the member states with a kind of bloc loyalty, which solidly implies that in each bloc there is a leading state, not only in terms of military supply, but also in terms of the determination of policy. To be sure, each bloc is riven with mounting internal tension. Economic competition divides the West, which enters the latest round of the arms race in a prolonged and, for some, mortifying slump. In the East, divergent interests are not so easily expressed, but they certainly exist, and from time to time become manifest. For all this, subordinate states on either side find it very difficult to stand off from their protectors.

But stand off we all must. The logic of preparation for a war in our 'theatre' is remorseless, and the profound worsening of tension between the superpowers at a time of world-wide economic and social crisis all serves to speed up the gadarene race …

Footnotes

1. *Apocalypse Now?* Spokesman, 1980, p. 3
2. F. Griffiths and J. C. Polanyi: *The Dangers of Nuclear War*, University of Toronto Press, 1980, 1980, p. 164.
3. Editorial, August 1980.
4. This speech is reproduced in full in *European Nuclear Disarmament: A Bulletin of Work in Progress* (Bertrand Russell Peace Foundation), No. 1, 1980.

The Zhukov File

An exchange of open letters with the Soviet Peace Committee

Yuri Zhukov
Ken Coates

The first Convention for European Nuclear Disarmament met in Brussels in 1982. Preparations for the second Convention, to be held in Berlin in May 1983, were under way when Mr Yuri Zhukov of the Soviet Peace Committee sent an open letter to all European Peace Movements. Ken Coates replied on behalf of the Russell Foundation. Both letters are reproduced in full.

I
The Soviet Peace Committee Criticises

36, Mira pr.
Moscow, USSR
December 1982

Dear Friends,

In our time as never before there is a need for a dialogue and mutual understanding among different peace forces.

We would like to share with you quite frankly some considerations about the prospects of the further development of the anti-war movement. We are prompted to do so by the disturbing development of the international situation.

The doctrine of a 'crusade' against the Soviet Union and the other socialist countries taken up as the official creed by the present US administration leads, in practical terms, not only to a direct confrontation in the political, ideological and economic spheres. The leaders of the USA and Nato openly proclaim plans of nuclear warfare.

In Europe, in spite of the arms limitation talks currently held, preparations are under way for deploying a new generation of US nuclear missiles. Evidence has come up to the effect that three to four times as many Pershing II and cruise missiles as were envisaged by Nato's 'double decision' of 1979 are being prepared for stationing. Moreover, the USA is intent on deploying Pershing II missiles, cruise missiles with nuclear warheads, and neutron weapons on the territory of Israel.

We believe the year 1983 when the deployment of US missiles in Western Europe is planned to begin to be especially important and in a sense crucial to the struggle for preventing this threat to peace and European security. And this is not just our view. More and more people in the West and in the East are becoming aware of the obvious truth that the dangerous international developments can only be stopped by joint and resolute mass actions of all those who are committed to peace. The anti-war movement everywhere is growing in strength and width and becoming an important factor of international politics, one that has to be heeded by all political parties and governments.

Yet, it is impossible to ignore the fact that there is a sharp increase in the actions by the opponents of peace forces, trying hard to neutralise the anti-war movement, disorientate the people in the movement and push them off the right way.

So far the peace champions of the various streams, movements and organisations both in the West and East have been coming out together for peace and disarmament, laying aside their ideological differences, however serious they might be. It is easy to see how much weaker their combined efforts would be if the anti-war movements were to set those differences as lines of demarcation between themselves, breeding enmity.

In this context one cannot but feel concerned about the discussions imposed by some persons and groups in order to eventually split the anti-war movement which is global by its nature and to infiltrate the 'cold war' elements into it. The promoters of those discussions increasingly strive to turn anti-war forums into an arena of open ideological struggle by replacing the discussion of the major task of preventing nuclear war, a task that united all, with debates on issues that have nothing to do with this task.

In this connection we would like to share with you our impressions of the Convention for European Nuclear Disarmament that was held in Brussels last July on the initiative of the Bertrand Russell Foundation and the so-called Movement for European Nuclear Disarmament (END). Its organisers claim that the purpose of this event was to 'rally the broad forces and groups within the mass anti-war movement on the basis of a wide discussion providing the groundwork for fruitful co-operation'. This concept of co-operation among the peace forces in Europe can only be welcomed. However, the deliberations and the outcome of the Brussels Convention have shown that the true objective of its sponsors was not to rally but to disunite the anti-war movements.

Prior to the Convention a lengthy discussion took place among its sponsors as to whether they should invite representatives of the public organisations of the socialist countries. Finally the participation issue was resolved so that the right to take part in the conference was granted not to the real mass peace movements of the socialist countries but to a group of people who have left their countries and have nothing in common with the struggle for peace and who, while representing nobody, are busy disseminating hostile slanderous fabrications about the foreign and home policies of their former motherland. Only as an exception were some representatives of Yugoslavia, Romania and Hungary allowed to attend.

As a result the Convention was a West European rather than a European operation for all its sponsors' insistence on the latter. This was the start of overt actions aimed at disuniting the anti-war movement in Europe.

These actions have caused perplexity and protests among many participants in the Convention. Indeed, one can hardly seriously believe that the struggle for peace and security in Europe can be successfully pursued without the participation of millions of people living in Europe's socialist countries. Whatever may be claimed by the organisers of the Convention on this score, they actually make an attempt to isolate the West European anti-war movements and organisations from the real mass movements of peace champions in the socialist countries and to substitute them by certain individuals passed off as allies who are active not in the struggle for détente and disarmament but in undermining the socialist system.

The Convention is known to have been held under the slogan of achieving European nuclear disarmament. It is also known that the only nuclear power which has made an official statement that it stands for elimination of all nuclear weapons from the whole European continent is the Soviet Union. Naturally the Soviet public organisations as well as all candid peace champions abroad welcome and support this stand. And yet there are people who try to practise discrimination against these organisations describing them as 'official' and 'dependent' on the grounds that they support the peace policy of their government.

We, as many other people, now query what are these people actually striving for – the elimination of nuclear weapons or rather the elimination of a united universal anti-war movement, the participation in which is determined both in the West and East not by anti or 'pro-government' stands but by its anti-militarist, anti-war positions.

It is a truly monstrous design to try and use the banner of peace in order to draw the anti-war movement into what is to all intents and purposes a 'cold war' against the public in socialist countries and to lead them along this path to the impasse of anti-Sovietism and anti-communism. These actions cannot be justified by the assertions of the Convention organisers that they wish to be 'neutral' to both 'superpowers' and strive to be equally removed from their foreign policies.

At present active preparations are known to be under way for the second Convention to be held in West Berlin in May 1983. We have hoped that its organisers would have analysed all negative aspects of the Brussels meeting and come up with a different, more democratic, politically balanced and responsible approach. In that case the Soviet public organisations which abide by the principle that co-operation must be sought among all peace forces with no exception, would have been ready to take part in the preparatory work and the deliberations of the Convention. That is why we agreed to hold consultative meetings with representatives of the West Berlin 'Working Group for a Nuclear-free Europe' who are in charge of the practical preparations for the second Convention.

We sincerely hoped that we would find, as a result of these meetings, a mutually acceptable basis for co-operation leading to a truly constructive dialogue between the peace forces representing not only the West but also the East at the Convention itself. However, contacts with the Convention organisers confirmed our worst apprehensions as to its character and orientation.

Our talks in Moscow in October 1982 with the representatives of the West Berlin 'Working Group for a Nuclear-free Europe' – J. Graalfs, W. Grunwald, G. Gumlich, T. Schweisfurth and R. Steinke – and the documents available to us made us quite certain that things boil down to a deliberate attempt to distract the attention of the peace-loving public away from the main source of deadly peril to the European nations, viz. plans to deploy a new generation of nuclear missiles in Western Europe in 1983. It has become obvious that the issue of a nuclear-free Europe is largely a rubber-stamp measure put on the agenda as a concession to the demands of really mass anti-war organisations working against the deployment of new US missiles.

The assertion of the organisers of the West Berlin Convention that they are intent on forming an 'anti-bloc' movement for 'equal responsibility of both blocs and above all, the USA and USSR, does not hold water. They wilfully elude any concrete analysis of the policies of certain states and hush up a well-known fact that the Warsaw Treaty Organisation has repeatedly made an official proposal to simultaneously dissolve both blocs and as for Nato leaders, they are reluctant even to discuss the matter.

The leaders of the Bertrand Russell Peace Foundation and the Movement for European Nuclear Disarmament somehow keep silent about the following significant fact. In a well-known Appeal for European Nuclear Disarmament of 28 April 1980, which is put forward as a political platform of the Convention, the authors have stated that both sides, i.e. the East and West, bear the equal blame and along with this they have appealed to the USA and USSR to remove all nuclear weapons from the European soil and specifically demanded that the USSR stop the production of Soviet medium-range SS20 missiles and the USA abandon its decision to deploy Pershing II and cruise missiles in Western Europe. They also appealed to both powers to ratify SALT II.

Since the publication of the Appeal the positions of the USSR and USA towards these demands have become definite. The USSR, as it has been mentioned, has come forward with a proposal of a real 'zero option' – to eliminate both medium-range weapons and tactical nuclear weapons from the European territory. It has stopped the stationing of medium-range missiles capable of hitting targets in Europe and even started a unilateral reduction of their quantity. The USSR has always been for the ratification and implementation of SALT II. Finally, the USSR has come out with a historic initiative pledging a unilateral obligation of non-use of nuclear weapons first.

However, the USA has taken an entirely opposite stand on all these issues, rejecting all the demands of the peace forces.

The leaders of the Bertrand Russell Foundation and the Movement for European Nuclear Disarmament make it appear that they are unaware of these facts and keep foisting on others their concept of 'equal responsibility'. We are firmly convinced that this concept is aimed at the disorientation, demobilisation and undermining of the anti-war movement and is called upon to conceal and justify an aggressive militarist policy of the USA and Nato.

It has become known that the organisers plan to bring a so-called 'German question' into discussions at the Convention, thus trying to challenge the inviolability of the post-war European frontiers and to violate the letter and spirit of the Helsinki Final Act.

The only way we can regard such political manoeuvres is as an attempt to revise the well-known agreements between the Federal Republic of Germany and its neighbours and the status of West Berlin.

It is not at all coincidental that the 'Working Group' is planning to hold an international symposium in West Berlin next June on the occasion of the 30th anniversary of the abortive counter-revolutionary coup staged in the GDR in 1953. What is it but an interference in the internal affairs of the GDR, and in effect a provocative attempt to force onto the anti-war movement an issue which has nothing to do with the movement for a nuclear-free Europe and resuscitates the revanchist sentiments.

We cannot agree with the anti-democratic stand taken by the organisers of the West Berlin Convention on the issue of preparation for this forum. We were told that the participation in the preparatory committee had been restricted only to those who adhere to the above Appeal incorporating a number of provisions unacceptable to many anti-war organisations, including ourselves. Moreover, as it has been shown above, some of the provisions of the Appeal are simply outdated. While clinging to this condition, the organisers of the Convention obviously try to use it for a selective approach in choosing the would-be participants among the individuals and organisations.

Answering the question of the possibility for the Peace Committees of the socialist countries to participate in the Convention, the representatives of the West Berlin 'Working Group' have evasively declared that it is practically impossible to solve this question within the framework of the Liaison Committee. How are they going to organise an East-West dialogue at the Convention? It turned out that they intended to selectively send out personal invitations to individual public figures in the socialist countries to attend in 'personal capacity' even then confining them to an observer status. This makes us certain that the Convention organisers simply fear the appearance of real opponents and therefore prefer to engage in anti-socialist propaganda in the absence of plenipotentiaries of public opinion in the Soviet Union and other socialist countries.

Neither can we agree with the fact that virtually all major decisions with regard to the preparations and proceedings at the Convention are taken by a limited group of people (K. Coates, L. Castellina, J. Lambert and J. Graalfs), while others are assigned the role of mute partners.

We are convinced that the orientation which the organisers try to lend to the Convention and the methods of its preparation preclude the possibility of a fruitful all-European dialogue, which would be conducive to expanding co-operation of peace forces, who hunger for it in the present menacing international situation. On the contrary, all this will contribute to fomenting a 'cold war' among the participants in the anti-war movement in Europe threatening to push this movement backwards. Naturally we shall not be a party to this wrecking undertaking.

We thought it necessary to let you know our stand with complete frankness so as to avoid misunderstanding or idle speculation. Our meetings and talks show that many public figures and organisations both in Eastern and Western Europe share our opinion or hold similar views with regard to the Convention.

For our part, we are going to continue working towards a better mutual understanding and joint actions of the public movements in the East and in the West for our common goal, that of averting the danger of nuclear war and freeing our continent of all nuclear weapons.

Your sincerely,
Yuri Zhukov,
President, Soviet Peace Committee.

II
The Russell Foundation Replies

1 February 1983

Dear Mr Zhukov,

We have just received your letter to Western Peace Movements, dated 2 December 1982. You did not send it to this Foundation, against which you raise serious complaints. We regret that you have not discussed these with us, since there are several points in which your letter errs, and which could have been clarified had you approached us. Now we are in the position of replying to an open letter, so we feel sure you will forgive us if we reply with a frankness equal to your own.

First, we must say that it is a pity that your letter so plainly contradicts the spirit of the important new initiatives taken by Mr Andropov and your Government during the past few weeks. During this time we have noted the very significant speech of 21 December, with its new offer concerning the further reduction of Soviet SS20 missiles against that of British and French equivalent weaponry. We find this entirely reasonable, and unequivocally support it. We also welcome the proposed 'no-first-use' agreement on conventional weapons, which we see as a worthwhile confidence-building measure. We further very much support the UN decision on a nuclear freeze, carried with your Government's adherence.

We also welcome new initiatives to normalise Soviet-Chinese relations. Not all, by any means, of these proposals are totally new in themselves, but as a package they give us real hope that a new policy in the USSR will re-open new and serious impulses to disarmament. In none of these matters are we your Government's critics. In fact, we think Mr Andropov has properly seized the initiative, and all pressure should be brought upon the United States and our own Government to reciprocate.

Yet, for all our hopes in this field, we still think that nonalignment is the proper course for our peace movements, and ultimately for all the European countries. This is not, as you wrongly assume, because we hold the two superpowers to be 'equally' responsible for the present state of the arms race. In fact we disagree with this view, and have frequently said so. Our main criticism has always been addressed to our own Government, against which we assert all our constitutional rights of opposition, because this is the main authority whose behaviour we may hope to influence. Nonetheless it is our opinion that blame of different kinds does historically attach to each bloc, and we do not wish simply to exchange blocs, but to make possible a genuine, and reciprocal, exit from the entire system of bloc divisions in our continent. In no way does this aspiration threaten the reasonable interests of the USSR, or the legitimate concerns of the USA. We seek amity with both powers in a changed world in which co-operation replaces conflict and the threat of the employment of force.

1983 is a crossroads for Europe and the world, as we have said consistently. The installation of the Pershing II and cruise missiles by Nato we see as a real threat to your country, which will within the logic of the arms race bring down further threats on our heads. Escalation of this already insane arms race imperils all mankind. That is the basis of our Appeal, although you never mention it.

What is your alternative? Our Appeal concerns the peoples of that Europe which is sandwiched between yourselves and the Americans. It must attract their majority support if it is to succeed. If your offer them peace instead on the sole basis of unswerving support for your own Government's policies in every field of world affairs, how many will agree? Obviously, this will depend in part on what those policies are. In the late 1950s and early '60s, your Government won many friends, who had originally been highly suspicious of the previous regime. One of these was our founder, Bertrand Russell, who recorded the progress of his thinking in his Autobiography:

'In the late '40s and early '50s, I had been profoundly impressed by the horror of Stalin's dictatorship, which had led me to believe that there would be no easy resolution of the cold war. I later came to see that for all his ruthlessness, Stalin had been very conservative. I had assumed, like most people in the West, that his tyranny was expansionist, but later evidence made it clear that it was the West that had given him Eastern Europe as part of the spoils of the Second World War, and that, for the most part, he had kept his agreements with the West. After his death, I earnestly hoped that the world would come to see the folly and danger of living permanently in the shadow of nuclear weapons. If the contenders for world supremacy could be kept apart, perhaps the neutral nations could introduce the voice of reason into international affairs. It was a small hope, for I overestimated the power of the neutrals. Only rarely, as with Nehru in Korea, did they manage to add significant weight to pressures against the cold war.

The neutrals continued to embody my outlook, in that I consider human survival more important than ideology. But a new danger came to the fore. It became obvious that Russia no longer entertained hope of world-empire, but that this hope had now passed over to the United States. As my researches into the origins and circumstances of the war in Vietnam showed, the United States was embarking upon military adventures which increasingly replaced war with Russia as the chief threat to the world. The fanaticism of America's anti-communism, combined with its constant search for markets and raw materials, made it impossible for any serious neutral to regard America and Russia as equally dangerous to the world.'

Russell's view of Soviet policy was subsequently partially changed again, mainly by the invasion of Czechoslovakia, which did much to distance you from many over here who want peace, and also from socialists and communists in many countries. Foreign reactions to the Soviet Union are only partly conditioned by bellicose propaganda, which is undoubtedly powerful, and from the attentions of which we suffer also. They are also formed by what your Government positively does. Now the Soviet Union is one of the major powers, not a besieged island attempting to pioneer new social forms. Paradoxically this means you can no longer rely on the uncritical support which was widely aroused in the earlier, embattled and heroic days of the foundation of your State. Today a peace movement composed of only your uncritical admirers in the West would consist of relatively few people, who would in no way constitute a force adequate to prevent the installation of cruise and Pershing II missiles, or to compel the United States and others to negotiate seriously to reverse the arms race. To fulfil these tasks, only a non-aligned movement has any hope of generating support on a wide enough scale. And the price of a non-aligned movement is that it is not aligned. The more constructively your Government is able to behave, the more such a movement will support you. The stronger it becomes, the more scope you will have for such constructive behaviour.

Thus, unless you were perversely to wish, for doctrinal reasons or whyever, to be able to act as arbitrarily and unkindly as possible, you ought to hope against hope that the non-aligned movement will grow. It is genuinely in both our interests. Not only may it help bring disarmament nearer, but it may also create more favourable conditions within which you may concentrate on your own peaceful renewal, and on carrying through safely and in optimal conditions whatever reforms you may think desirable and progressive. A non-aligned movement all over Europe, with millions of supporters, would mean that we, too, recovered a freedom of action which has been denied to us whilst our predominant modes of thought have been locked into the blocs. In what imaginable way does this threaten you? How does it 'provoke' you? As you rightly say, the Soviet Union has many times affirmed such a European perspective as its own. Why, when we assert it, and seek to give it material embodiment, does it suddenly 'divide the peace movement' and serve the interests of Nato?

Some people over here accuse us of precisely the opposite intentions. In our peace movements, as you know, there exist many different minorities, and much dissent, about some of which you are well informed. We will happily assist you to gain even fuller information, if you would like it. This dissent is our strength. It enables pacifists, socialists, church people, communists, greens and all kinds of special groups to work together, not simply, as you put it, 'laying aside' their differences, but actually celebrating those differences in common cause. Such differences will be plainly apparent, in profusion, at the Berlin Convention next May. That is why we invited you to come, to share in the experience, and to discuss with us. All of us will learn from it.

But why, then, could we not ask you to co-organise the event? Because it is organised by signatories of the April 1980 Appeal which your letter misunderstands and indeed denounces. The agenda is our agenda, an agenda of non-alignment. Whilst we have already informed you that we would welcome you among us, you must surely appreciate that we cannot surrender our own joint control over what is our platform. Do you always expect people to agree to such conditions when you visit them? If so, your travels must be rather restricted. The fraternal delegates of the CPSU do not tell the British Labour Party Conference that they must be invited to serve on the Conference Arrangements Committee before they will come, and Soviet Trade Unions are quite willing to visit other trade union bodies without making any demands whatever upon them. Why do you believe that the Peace Movement should be an exception to this rule? Surely there is no doubt about what you would say if we requested reciprocal rights concerning the agenda of your own meetings? No, this is not a serious proposal. We are what we are, and you are what you are, and we are willing to talk if you find it useful. But if we offer you friendship, it would be friendship without subservience.

Now let me deal with detailed matters on which you are wrongly informed. Your report our discussion about Eastern European participation at Brussels, saying that we invited 'a group of people who have left their countries and have nothing in common with the struggle for peace and who, while representing nobody, are busy disseminating hostile slanderous fabrications about the foreign and home policies of their former motherland'. Which people are these? We do not know them. We in fact invited all signatories to our Appeal. One of these is Zhores Medvedev, who was the only Russian to speak in a panel discussion. So far was he from 'disseminating hostile slanderous fabrications' about the USSR, that many of the European communists who were present thought he was unduly supportive of official Soviet positions. This was not our view, since we shared most of his reasoning. It is difficult to see how you could have arrived at the view expressed in your letter, had you been aware of what Dr Medvedev actually said.

'Only as an exception', you say, were some representatives of Yugoslavia 'allowed to attend'. This is far from the truth. The Yugoslav League for Peace, Independence and Equality of Peoples was among the earlier signatories to our Appeal, and they participated, and will participate, as of right in all our deliberations. They honoured us by sending their immediate past President, Bogdan Osolnik, together with another member of their presidency. As the premier non-aligned peace movement in Europe, they have our deep respect. Also present were distinguished Romanian and Hungarian participants, both of whom played an active and very constructive role in the workshops they chose to attend. Ask them. If their experiences are evidence of 'overt actions aimed at disuniting the anti-war movement' then it would be difficult to see how to strive for peace on any basis other than one which would reduce all the European movements to miniscule proportions. Since neither we nor you want that, we had better think again.

You make much of the alleged preoccupation of our forthcoming Convention with the 'German Question'. In fact there is no such preoccupation. The Liaison Committee has allocated one seminar amongst two dozen or so to the consideration of the issue of German Disarmament, which is raised by some

German peace activists, not as a slogan of revanchism, but as a call for the denuclearisation of both Germanies. Is this such a bad idea? If so, will the fact not become apparent in a free and open discussion? How do you imagine a mass peace movement can reach consensus about its goals without such exchanges? Concerning the meeting of 17 June of which you speak, we know nothing. Our Convention is scheduled from 9 May to 15 May. We are not involved in any subsequent gathering. If you had asked us, you would instantly have discovered this fact.

Then you go on to criticise the organisation of the Liaison Committee which organises the Convention. Here your remarks are equally ill-informed. This Committee involves nearly a hundred people from more than a score of countries. It controls the Conventions in every detail. The four joint secretaries who you name do not meet separately, have no special powers, and are charged solely with the convening of meetings. Why does all this alarm you? It is a completely transparent process, both in its unity and its diversity. If you allow yourself to feel threatened by it, you are suffering from empty phobias.

We do not wish here to exchange detailed opinions about which particular aspects of Soviet policy merit support, and which opposition. One day, we hope, we will talk about it. But we should also talk about your misperception of our own attitudes to the many wrongs done in the 'Western' part of the world. Surely you cannot have been at your desk at *Pravda* for as long as you have been without being aware of some aspects or other of our own consistent opposition to all forms of imperialism, of our efforts to assist colonial struggles for independence, or of our general defence of civil freedoms and political prisoners in countries East, West and Neutral.

Your letter does your Committee a disservice by offering such unsubtle attempts to represent us as *agents provocateurs* in the service of the Western powers. We have no doubt that you will quickly be disabused of these opinions when you begin to receive replies from those to whom you have addressed your remarks. They will provoke dismay among many of your well-wishers.

Now we begin a new year. Let us propose that instead of writing *about* each other, we write *to* each other, and see what emerges.

Yours sincerely,
Ken Coates

Palestine Tragedy

Bertrand Russell

Bertrand Russell's last message, to an international conference of Parliamentarians meeting in Cairo, addressed the crisis in the Middle East. It was published in the second number of The Spokesman, *shortly after his death in 1970.*

The latest phase of the undeclared war in the Middle East is based upon a profound miscalculation. The bombing raids deep into Egyptian territory will not persuade the civilian population to surrender, but will stiffen their resolve to resist. This is the lesson of all aerial bombardment. The Vietnamese who have endured years of American heavy bombing have responded not by capitulation but by shooting down more enemy aircraft. In 1940 my own fellow countrymen resisted Hitler's bombing raids with an unprecedented unity and determination. For this reason, the present Israeli attacks will fail in their essential purpose, but at the same time they must be condemned vigorously throughout the world.

The development of the crisis in the Middle East is both dangerous and instructive. For over 20 years Israel has expanded by force of arms. After every stage in this expansion Israel has appealed to 'reason' and has suggested 'negotiations'. This is the traditional role of the imperial power, because it wishes to consolidate with the least difficulty what it has taken already by violence. Every new conquest becomes the new basis of the proposed negotiations from strength, which ignores the injustice of the previous aggression. The aggression committed by Israel must be condemned, not only because no state has the right to annexe foreign territory, but because every expansion is also an experiment to discover how much more aggression the world will tolerate.

The refugees who surround Palestine in their hundreds of thousands were described recently by the Washington journalist I. F. Stone as 'the moral millstone around the neck of world Jewry'. Many of the refugees are now well into the third decade of their precarious existence in temporary settlements. The tragedy of the people of Palestine is that their country was 'given' by a foreign Power to another people for the creation of a new State. The result was that many hundreds of thousands of innocent people were made permanently homeless. With every new conflict their numbers have increased. How much longer is the world willing to endure this spectacle of wanton cruelty? It is abundantly clear that the refugees have every right to the homeland from which they were driven, and the denial of this right is at the heart of the continuing conflict. No people anywhere in the world would accept being expelled *en masse* from their own country; how can anyone require the people of Palestine to accept a punishment which nobody else would tolerate? A permanent just settlement of the refugees in their homelands is an essential ingredient of any genuine settlement in the Middle East.

We are frequently told that we must sympathise with Israel because of the suffering of the Jews in Europe at the hands of the Nazis. I see in this suggestion no reason to perpetuate any suffering. What Israel is doing today cannot be condoned, and to invoke the horrors of the past to justify those of the present is gross hypocrisy. Not only does Israel condemn a vast number of refugees to misery; not only are many Arabs under occupation condemned to military rule; but also Israel condemns the Arab nations only recently emerging from colonial status, to continuing impoverishment as military demands take precedence over national development.

All who want to see an end to bloodshed in the Middle East must ensure that any settlement does not contain the seeds of future conflict. Justice requires that the first step towards a settlement must be an Israeli withdrawal from all the territories occupied in June 1967. A new world campaign is needed to help bring justice to the long-suffering people of the Middle East.

Fighting for Trade Union freedom

Build peace not bombs - no new Trident

Bob Crow
General Secretary

John Leach
President

Left Parties Everywhere

Oskar Lafontaine

Oskar Lafontaine served as Prime Minister of Saarland and President of the German Bundesrat. He was the SPD's candidate for Federal Chancellor in 1990, when a woman attacked and critically wounded him with a knife. In September 1998, he was appointed Federal Minister of Finance, but resigned the following March. In 2005, he left the SPD and founded the Left Party, which subsequently merged with the PDS, the successor to the Socialist Unity Party of Germany (SED) in the German Democratic Republic. Lafontaine is now joint Chairman of the merged Left Party (Die Linke). He recently gave an interview to the newspaper Neues Deutschland, *from which we reprint excerpts. The questions are in italics, and Mr Lafontaine's replies in ordinary type.*

Mr Lafontaine, since Die Linke was founded, not even so much as an historic blink of the eye has elapsed, and already the party has moved into four state assemblies in the West. It is on the point of becoming an all-German party, maybe even an all-German catch-all party. Did you think this success possible?

Two years ago I would not have thought that we could be so successful so quickly. Yet, apparently more and more people want politics in Germany to change. The policy of the grand coalition is marked by value added tax fraud, social decline, increasing the retirement age to 67, and involvement in wars in defiance of international law. The majority of people refuse this and see in Die Linke a new political force that counters it.

SPD Chair Kurt Beck said your party was an adversary. Is the SPD also an adversary to you?

Of course. Parties compete for voters. And in this respect the SPD is an adverse party, like other parties, too. Naturally, as the example of Hesse shows, there are overlapping features in the programmes of the SPD and Die Linke. After the elections, it would be natural for all parties involved to sit down together on the basis of what they said in their programmes and ask: where is the common ground and what is the best way to co-operate? The parties competing with us are not that mature at the moment.

Do you think Kurt Beck's course has a future in the SPD? Does the SPD have a future pursuing this course?

Originally Beck stood for a strategy that had to fail. It was that you can co-operate with Die Linke in the East but not in the West. It was certain that this strategy would not last. He has now corrected this mistake. Now we have to wait to see how things develop. Die Linke adheres to its fundamental statement: we want to change politics. And we are ready to co-operate with others on the basis of our programme.

Your party is accused of living in cloud-cuckoo-land: your programme is not financially affordable.

I only have to say one sentence: not a single cut in welfare services would have been necessary in the past few years if we had the average European tax rate, which is about 40%. Ours is 35%. I promised each journalist, each professor and each politician a gold watch if they managed to refute that statement. So far I have not yet had to give away any gold watches; that means the objections of our adversaries are wrong, knowing the figures …

Quite often it is questioned that you are on the left. Are you?

What is left? I have a simple answer: Left is when you side with the employees, the pensioners, and the socially needy, when in doubt. That is what we do. And I do, too.

Cue 25 April 1990. Do you still remember that day? Do you dream about it?

That was the day an attempt was made on my life. That was 18 years ago, and I think I have come to grips with it to a large degree. During the first years, it kept me more on my toes. What was decisive for me was that I recognised one always has to live in a way so one can say I did things right, because tomorrow life can be over.

Do you manage?

When it comes to my own demands and yardsticks, yes. It is important to me that you should treat people the way you would like to be treated yourself. This is also a short programme for Die Linke.

Nevertheless, your life is inseparably linked to social democracy, is it not? In 1985, you became the first Social Democratic Prime Minister of the Saarland, and in 1990 you ran for Chancellor. In 1995 you were elected party chair. Does your heart still beat for the SPD, the SPD as it once was? Or have you found a new political home in Die Linke, which you co-founded?

When it comes to the SPD, membership always meant commitment to programmes and political ideas. The party was not a club such as a choir or sports club, but rather an association used to achieve political goals. Willy Brandt described one pivotal goal: peace. When he received the Nobel Peace Prize he called war the *ultima irratio* in his speech. These days the SPD again says war is the *ultima ratio*. I stick with Willy Brandt's sentence: war is the *ultima irratio*. My heart still beats for this sentence.

On the other hand, I have a hand in founding Die Linke. It takes a lot of work, heart and soul. Die Linke is my political home now. It is already about to change German politics, and this is very important to us.

Why do you think today's SPD has veered so far away from Willy Brandt's SPD?

The heart of the matter for the Left is to what extent does it manage not to fall for the temptations and seductions of capitalist power structures? The SPD did not manage to do so, resulting in leading social democratic politicians ending up with some private equity firms or major gas consortiums. Still, some decades ago this would have been unimaginable. Brandt and Wehner in a private equity firm or temporary employment company? Unthinkable …

What is your goal? Do you want to unite both parties, Die Linke and the SPD, one day?

This question is often raised. Yet, the SPD and Die Linke are completely different. Without a doubt there is only time for one thing: German politics needs a left party. Not only German politics, but also European politics, because the formerly socialist and social democratic parties have been pocketed by neoliberalism over the past few years. If you want a social renewal you need new left parties everywhere. No things can grow together that do not belong together.

You once said Die Linke now stood for the SPD programme which had still met with much approval from the voters in 1989. You were head of the commission then, which drew up the social democratic principles that are known as the Berlin programme. Almost 20 years have passed. Is this programme still timely? Do programmes not have to change, inevitably?

Yes and No. If the programme includes giving employees and pensioners a decent share of the increase in prosperity, this is timeless. The same applies to the pension formula that avoids poverty in old age. And saying that we need a foreign policy that respects international law, and never gets involved in wars in defiance of international law, as was the basis for the SPD programme in the times of Willy Brandt, this is timeless as well. Sometimes it is really aggravating to see that such principles are treated as if they are no longer modern. There are programme principles of Die Linke that are as constant as the guarantee of human rights by the Basic Law (constitution). Yet, certainly each time needs its new answers. Let's take the discussion on the general strike or mass strike, which Die Linke has triggered in Germany. Such positions were neither discussed by the SPD nor the Socialist Unity Party of Germany (SED) in the past. And talking about an ecological renewal today, and making re-municipalising a programme principle of Die Linke, and noting with surprise that other parties pick up on the subject of re-municipalising energy suppliers, this is very much an answer of the present time. Thirty or forty years ago, energy supply was still a municipal business. Later it was more and more privatised. Now we say that step was wrong and correct it. It stands out particularly in this place how thoughtless the argument is that you cannot suggest anything that used to exist some time ago ...

Once again about your election successes, you personally are said to be for involvement in government. Is that true?

That always makes me laugh because when you add up all the times I probably was in government longest in Germany including the time as Mayor of Saarbrücken. My position is clear. If you can accomplish your own policies, you have to enter government. If not, you must try to do so in opposition. We, Die Linke, are particular proof of the fact that a relatively small political force can change politics as an opposition party.

After Hiroshima

Kevin Rudd

The Prime Minister of Australia made Hiroshima his first port of call during his visit to Japan in June 2008. Later, in Kyoto, he announced a new International Commission on Nuclear Non-Proliferation and Disarmament, to revive the work pioneered by the Canberra Commission on the Elimination of Nuclear Weapons in the 1990s (see Maj Britt Theorin's 'Is a nuclear-weapons-free world achievable?' in Spokesman 98*). These excerpts are taken from his speech.*

In the past decade, the world has not paid adequate attention to nuclear weapons.

There have been nuclear developments that we have had to confront – like North Korea's nuclear programme and the danger it poses to the region; as well as Iran's continued nuclear ambitions.

And there has been some thinking about new ways to counter the threat of weapons proliferation. Australia and Japan were both founding partners in the Proliferation Security Initiative (PSI). And Australia and Japan cooperate closely on export controls in the Nuclear Suppliers Group (NSG). These help to support the cornerstone of the global effort to eliminate nuclear weapons – in particular the Nuclear Non-Proliferation Treaty (NPT).

But there has not been the same focus on the danger of nuclear weapons that we saw at the height of the Cold War. In some ways that is understandable – nuclear weapon stockpiles have come down a long way since their peaks in the 1980s. The two main nuclear powers, our shared ally the United States and Russia, have negotiated a series of treaties that have cut the number of nuclear weapons.

And South Africa and Ukraine have shown that it is possible for countries that have nuclear weapons to eliminate them.

We no longer live with the daily fear of nuclear war between two superpowers. But nuclear weapons remain. New states continue to seek to acquire them. Some states including in our own region are expanding their existing capacity.

Hiroshima reminds us of the terrible power of these weapons. Hiroshima should remind us that we must be vigilant afresh to stop their continued proliferation. And we must be committed to the ultimate objective of a nuclear weapons free world.

The cornerstone of the global nuclear disarmament efforts remains the Nuclear Non-Proliferation Treaty (NPT). It is a treaty that is grounded in the reality of the existence of nuclear weapons, but with a firm goal of their eventual elimination. It is a treaty that, by any historical measure, has helped arrest the spread of nuclear weapons – particularly given the proliferation pressures that existed across states in the 1960s when the treaty was negotiated.

But 40 years later the treaty is under great pressure. Some states have developed nuclear weapons outside the treaty's framework. Some, like North Korea, have defied the international community and have stated that they have left the treaty altogether. Others like Iran defy the content of the treaty by continuing to defy the International Atomic Energy Agency – the agency assigned to give the treaty force.

There are two courses of action available to the community of nations: to allow the NPT to continue to fragment; or to exert every global effort to restore and defend the treaty. Australia stands unambiguously for the treaty.

I accept fully that we have a difficult task ahead of us. But I believe Japan and Australia working together can make a difference in the global debate on proliferation. We are uniquely qualified. Japan remains the only state to have experienced the consequences of nuclear weapons. Japan today has a large nuclear power industry. Australia has the largest known uranium reserves in the world. We can, therefore, understand the concerns that countries bring to this debate. And we share a view of the importance of the NPT. Australia and Japan are also both recognised as being committed to non-proliferation, including through our strong support for the International Atomic Energy Agency.

Each year, for more than a decade, Japan has put forward a UN resolution on nuclear disarmament. Each year, Australia is proud to be a co-sponsor of that resolution. We do more than just vote for it. Alongside Japan we present it to the international community and jointly seek their support.

Australia itself for the last quarter century has developed strong global credentials in arms control and disarmament – through our establishment of the Australia Group; our work in the United Nations on the Chemical Weapons Convention and as one of its original signatories; and our work on the Comprehensive Nuclear Test Ban Treaty.

Australia and Japan have also both been at the forefront of global thinking on the long-term challenge of nuclear weapons. In the 1990s, Australia convened the Canberra Commission on the Elimination of Nuclear Weapons. Japan in the late 1990s established the Tokyo Forum for Nuclear Non-Proliferation and Disarmament. These two bodies produced reports that have become benchmarks in the international community's efforts to deal with nuclear weapons.

I think it is time we looked anew at the questions they addressed and revisited some of the conclusions they reached. The NPT Review Conference will be held in 2010. It is the five yearly meeting of parties to the treaty to assess progress against the treaty's aims and look at how we can strengthen its provisions.

As former US Secretary of State Henry Kissinger said in 2007, nuclear non-proliferation is the most important issue facing the world today. So, before we get to the Review Conference, we need to do some serious thinking about how we support the treaty and how we move forward on our goals.

I announce today that Australia proposes to establish an International Commission on Nuclear Non-Proliferation and Disarmament, to be co-chaired by former Australian foreign minister Gareth Evans. The Commission will re-examine the Canberra Commission and the Tokyo Forum reports to see how far we have come, how much work remains, and develop a possible plan of action for the future. The Commission will report to a major international conference of experts in late 2009 that will be sponsored by Australia. I look forward to discussing with Japan their participation in the work of this Commission.

Australia and Japan have also agreed to establish a high-level dialogue on non-proliferation and disarmament to advance this critical international debate. It is intended that the Commission and the subsequent conference will help pave the way for the NPT Review Conference in 2010. We cannot simply stand idly by and allow another Review Conference to achieve no progress – or worse to begin to disintegrate. The treaty is too important. The goal of nuclear non-proliferation is too important.

Even with these additional efforts, there is no guarantee of success. But that should not deter us from exerting every diplomatic effort. This is a view shared by people with unique experience in strategic policy. In the United States, former Secretaries of State George Shultz and Henry Kissinger, former Defence Secretary William Perry, and former Chairman of the US Senate Armed Services Committee Sam Nunn said in an important article the *Wall Street Journal* in January:

> 'The accelerating spread of nuclear weapons, nuclear know-how and nuclear material has brought us to a nuclear tipping point. … The steps we are taking now to address these threats are not adequate to the danger.'

Relevant to our deliberations here, this eminent group of Americans has suggested steps for the future. They have said we should:

- strengthen the means of monitoring compliance with the NPT – which could be achieved through requiring all NPT signatories to adopt monitoring provisions designed by the International Atomic Energy Agency;
- develop an international system to manage the nuclear fuel cycle – given the growing interest in nuclear energy; and
- adopt a process to bring the Comprehensive Nuclear Test Ban Treaty into force.

It is time for a new approach – of which the revitalisation of the Nuclear Non-Proliferation Treaty and the International Atomic Energy Agency is a critical part.

The Surge
A Balance Sheet

William E. Odom

Lt. General Odom, US Army (Ret.), gave this testimony before the Senate Foreign Relations Committee on Iaq on 2 April 2008. He was formerly the Director of the National Security Agency.

The last occasion [I appeared before the committee] was in January 2007, when the topic was the troop surge. Today you are asking if it has worked.

Last year I rejected the claim that it was a new strategy. Rather, I said, it is a new tactic used to achieve the same old strategic aim, political stability. And I foresaw no serious prospects for success.

I see no reason to change my judgment now. The surge is prolonging instability, not creating the conditions for unity as the president claims.

Last year, General Petraeus wisely declined to promise a military solution to this political problem, saying that he could lower the level of violence, allowing a limited time for the Iraqi leaders to strike a political deal. Violence has been temporarily reduced but today there is credible evidence that the political situation is far more fragmented. And currently we see violence surge in Baghdad and Basra. In fact, it has also remained sporadic and significant in several other parts of Iraq over the past year, notwithstanding the notable drop in Baghdad and Anbar Province.

More disturbing, Prime Minister Maliki has initiated military action and then dragged in US forces to help his own troops destroy his Shiite competitors. This is a political setback, not a political solution. Such is the result of the surge tactic.

No less disturbing has been the steady violence in the Mosul area, and the tensions in Kirkuk between Kurds, Arabs, and Turkomen. A showdown over control of the oil fields there surely awaits us. And the idea that some kind of a federal solution can cut this Gordian knot strikes me as a wild fantasy, wholly out of touch with Kurdish realities.

Also disturbing is Turkey's military incursion to destroy Kurdish PKK groups in the border region. That confronted the US government with a choice: either to support its Nato ally, or to make good on its commitment to Kurdish leaders to insure their security. It chose the former, and that makes it clear to the Kurds that the United States will sacrifice their security to its larger interests in Turkey.

Turning to the apparent success in Anbar province and a few other Sunni areas, this is not the positive situation it is purported to be. Certainly violence has declined as local Sunni sheikhs have begun to co-operate with US forces. But the surge tactic cannot be given full credit. The decline started earlier on Sunni initiative. What are their motives? First, anger at Al Qaeda operatives and second, their financial plight. Their break with Al Qaeda should give us little comfort. The Sunnis welcomed anyone who would help them kill Americans, including Al Qaeda. The concern we hear the President and his aides express, about a residual base left for Al Qaeda if we withdraw, is utter nonsense. The Sunnis will soon destroy Al Qaeda if we leave Iraq.

The Kurds do not allow them in their region, and the Shiites, like the Iranians, detest Al Qaeda. To understand why, one need only take note of the Al Qaeda public diplomacy campaign over the past year or so on internet blogs. They implore the United States to bomb and invade Iran and destroy this apostate Shiite regime. As an aside, it gives me pause to learn that our Vice President and some members of the Senate are aligned with Al Qaeda on spreading the war to Iran.

Let me emphasize that our new Sunni friends insist on being paid for their loyalty. I have heard, for example, a rough estimate that the cost in one area of about 100 square kilometers is $250,000 per day. And periodically they threaten to defect unless their fees are increased. You might want to find out the total costs for these deals forecasted for the next several years, because they are not small and they do not promise to end. Remember, we do not own these people. We merely rent them. And they can break the lease at any moment. At the same time, this deal protects them to some degree from the government's troops and police, hardly a sign of political reconciliation.

Now let us consider the implications of the proliferating deals with the Sunni strongmen. They are far from unified among themselves. Some remain with Al Qaeda. Many who break and join our forces are beholden to no one. Thus the decline in violence reflects a dispersion of power to dozens of local strongmen who distrust the government and occasionally fight among themselves. Thus the basic military situation is far worse because of the proliferation of armed groups under local military chiefs who follow a proliferating number of political bosses.

This can hardly be called greater military stability, much less progress toward political consolidation, and to call it fragility that needs more time to become success is to ignore its implications. At the same time, Prime Minister Maliki's military actions in Basra and Baghdad indicate even wider political and military fragmentation. We are witnessing what is more accurately described as the road to the Balkanization of Iraq, that is, political fragmentation. We are being asked by the President to believe that this shift of so much power and finance to so many local chieftains is the road to political centralization. He describes the process as building the state from the bottom up.

I challenge you to press the administration's witnesses this week to explain this absurdity. Ask them to name a single historical case where power has been aggregated successfully from local strongmen to a central government except through bloody violence leading to a single winner, most often a dictator. That is the history of feudal Europe's transformation to the age of absolute monarchy. It is the story of the American colonization of the west and our Civil War. It took England 800 years to subdue clan rule on what is now the English-Scottish border. And it is the source of violence in Bosnia and Kosovo.

How can our leaders celebrate this diffusion of power as effective state building? More accurately described, it has placed the United States astride several civil wars. And it allows all sides to consolidate, rearm, and refill their financial coffers at the US expense. To sum up, we face a deteriorating political situation with an over-extended army. When the administration's witnesses appear before you, you should make them clarify how long the army and marines can sustain this band-aid strategy.

The only sensible strategy is to withdraw rapidly but in good order. Only that step can break the paralysis now gripping US strategy in the region. The next step is to choose a new aim, regional stability, not a meaningless victory in Iraq. And progress toward that goal requires revising our policy toward Iran. If the President merely renounced his threat of regime change by force, that could prompt Iran to lessen its support to Taliban groups in Afghanistan. Iran detests the Taliban and supports them only because they will kill more Americans in Afghanistan as retaliation in event of a US attack on Iran. Iran's policy toward Iraq would also have to change radically as we withdraw. It cannot want instability there. Iraqi Shiites are Arabs, and they know that Persians look down on them. Co-operation between them has its limits.

No quick reconciliation between the US and Iran is likely, but US steps to make Iran feel more secure make it far more conceivable than a policy calculated to increase its insecurity. The President's policy has reinforced Iran's determination to acquire nuclear weapons, the very thing he purports to be trying to prevent. Withdrawal from Iraq does not mean withdrawal from the region. It must include a realignment and reassertion of US forces and diplomacy that give us a better chance to achieve our aim. A number of reasons are given for not withdrawing soon and completely. I have refuted them repeatedly before but they have more lives than a cat. Let me try again to explain why they don't make sense.

First, it is insisted that we must leave behind military training elements with no combat forces to secure them. This makes no sense at all. The idea that US military trainers left alone in Iraq can be safe and effective is flatly rejected by several NCOs and junior officers I have heard describe their personal experiences. Moreover, training foreign forces before they have a consolidated political authority to command their loyalty is a windmill tilt. Finally, Iraq is not short on military skills.

Second, it is insisted that chaos will follow our withdrawal. We heard that argument as the 'domino theory' in Vietnam. Even so, the path to political stability will be bloody regardless of whether we withdraw or not. The idea that the United States has a moral responsibility to prevent this ignores that reality. We are certainly to blame for it, but we do not have the physical means to prevent it. American leaders who insist that it is in our power to do so are misleading both the public and themselves if they believe it. The real moral question is whether to risk the lives of more Americans. Unlike preventing chaos, we have the physical means to stop sending more troops where many will be killed or wounded. That is the moral responsibility to our country which no American leaders seems willing to assume.

Third, nay-sayers insist that our withdrawal will create regional instability. This confuses cause with effect. Our forces in Iraq and our threat to change Iran's regime are making the region unstable. Those who link instability with a US withdrawal have it exactly backwards. Our ostrich strategy of keeping our heads buried in the sands of Iraq has done nothing but advance our enemies' interest. I implore you to reject these fallacious excuses for prolonging the commitment of US forces to war in Iraq.

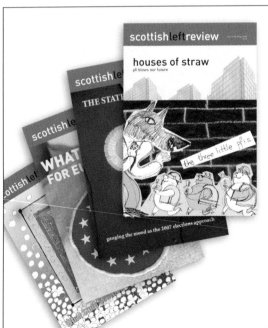

TRIDENT is aimed at coercion, causes destruction and divides our world.

AID sets its sights on making friends, spreading peace and encouraging development.

Which is the civilized choice?

Keith Norman
General Secretary

Alan Donnelly
President

ASLEF the train drivers' union
www.aslef.org.uk

Unite - the union
Derek Simpson and Tony Woodley
Joint General Secretaries

www.unitetheunion.com

Solidarity with Cuba

Free the
Miami Five

THE BERTRAND RUSSELL PEACE FOUNDATION
DOSSIER

2008   Number 28

RUSSELL TRIBUNAL ON PALESTINE

Preparations for the Tribunal continue, as this new bulletin shows.

We call for the creation of a Russell Tribunal on Palestine. This Tribunal will work rigorously and in the same spirit as the Tribunal on Vietnam that sat in 1967, under the presidency of Jean-Paul Sartre. The Tribunal will have to judge the breaches of international law, of which the Palestinians are victims, and which deprive the Palestinian people of a sovereign State.

The Advisory Opinion given by the International Court of Justice of The Hague on the 9th of July, 2004 sums up those violations, and concludes, in particular, with the obligation for Israel to dismantle the Wall and to compensate the Palestinians for all the damage suffered from its construction. This Opinion recalls, in its §163,D, that 'All States are under an obligation not to recognise the illegal situation resulting from the construction of the wall and not to render aid or assistance in maintaining the situation created by such construction; all State parties to the Fourth Geneva Convention relative to the Protection of Civilian Persons in Time of War of the 12th of August 1949 have in addition the obligation, while respecting the United Nations Charter and international law, to ensure compliance by Israel with international law as embodied in that Convention'.

This Opinion has been confirmed on the 24th of July 2004, by the resolution ES-10/15 of the General Assembly of the United Nations, adopted by 150 Member States. The General Assembly 'demands that Israel, the occupying Power, comply with its legal obligations as mentioned in the advisory opinion' and 'calls upon all States Members of the United Nations to comply with their legal obligations as mentioned in the advisory opinion'.

Drawing in particular on the Advisory Opinion and the UN resolution, the Russell Tribunal on Palestine will reaffirm the primacy of international law as the basis for the settlement of the Israeli Palestinian conflict. It will identify breaches to the application of the law and will condemn all the perpetrators before international public opinion. Your support of this Tribunal will give it the moral weight necessary to advance the cause of justice and law in this part of the world. Thanking you for you attention and your response to this appeal, and with cordial greetings.

Ken Coates, Chairman of the Bertrand Russell Peace Foundation, **Nurit Peled,** Sakharov Prize 2001, **Leila Shahid,** General Delegate of Palestine to the European Union, Belgium, Luxembourg

'May this Tribunal **prevent the crime of silence**[1]'... declared Bertrand Russell to define the spirit and the objective of the International War Crimes Tribunal constituted in 1966 to investigate crimes committed in Vietnam and judge them according to international law. Initiated by Lord Russell, who was awarded the Nobel Prize for Literature in 1950, and supported by eminent intellectuals such as Jean-Paul Sartre, who chaired the Tribunal, Lelio Basso, Günther Anders, James Baldwin, Simone de Beauvoir, Lazaro Cardenas, Stokely Carmichael, Isaac Deutscher, Gisèle Halimi, Laurent Schwartz ... this Tribunal was named the Russell Tribunal.

The Russell Tribunal has no legal character but acts as a court of the people, a Tribunal of conscience, faced with injustices and violations of international law, that are not dealt with by existing international jurisdictions, or that are recognised but continue with complete impunity due to the lack of political will of the international community.

Today, and in the same spirit, the Bertrand Russell Foundation supports the setting up of a Russell Tribunal to examine the violations of international law, of which the Palestinians are victims, and that prevent the Palestinian People from exercising their rights to a sovereign State.

This Tribunal has been named the Russell Tribunal on Palestine. It will reaffirm the supremacy of international law as the basis for a solution to the Israeli Palestinian conflict. It will identify all the failings to the implementation of this right, and will condemn all the parties responsible for these failings, in full view of international public opinion.

It will thus examine the various responsibilities that lead to the persistence of the occupation of the Palestinian Territories by Israel and the non-application of the United Nations resolutions, from Resolution 181 of the 29th of November 1947, on the partition of Palestine, to the Resolution ES-10/15 of the 20th of July 2004, that acknowledges the Opinion of the International Court of Justice (ICJ) – of the 9th of July 2004 – on the construction of the Wall by Israel in the Occupied Palestinian Territories and requests all the UN Member States to acquit themselves of their legal obligations as defined by the ICJ Opinion. The responsibilities of Israel and also of other states, particularly the United States and the Member States of the European Union, the Arab States and the international organizations concerned (United Nations, the European Union, the Arab League) will be scrutinised.

The Tribunal also aims, by this approach, to contribute to the mobilisation and involvement of civil society in all the states concerned with the question of Palestine.

The Russell Tribunal on Palestine is composed of personalities from all states, including Israel, which will be one of the states investigated. The legitimacy of the Russell Tribunal on Palestine does not come from a government or any political party but from the prestige, professional interests and commitment to fundamental rights of the Members that constitute this Tribunal.

Members of the Support Committee (2008)

Madam Nguyen Thi Bin Former Vice-President, Vietnam, **Ahmed Ben Bella** First President, Algeria, **Milan Kucan** Former President, Slovenia, **Andreas Van**

Agt Former Prime Minister, Netherlands, **Tariq Ali** Writer, UK, **Henri Alleg** Journalist, France, **Martin Almada** Lawyer, Writer, Right Livelihood Award 2002, Paraguay, **Kader Asmal** Professor, Former Minister, MP, South Africa, **Raymond Aubrac (and Lucie Aubrac †)** Former Members of the French Resistance, France, **Etienne Balibar** Professor Emeritus, France, **Anna Balletbo** President of Fundació Internacional Olof Palme, Spain, **Russell Banks** Writer, USA, **Mohammed Bedjaoui** Former President of the International Court of Justice (The Hague), Former Minister of Foreign Affairs, Algeria, **Amar Bentoumi** President Emeritus of the International Association of Democratic Lawyers, Algeria, **John Berger** Writer, UK, **Howard Brenton** Writer, UK, **Carmel Budiardjo** Right Livelihood Award 1995, UK, **Judith Butler** Professor, USA, **Monique Chemillier-Gendreau** Professor Emeritus, France, **Noam Chomsky** Professor MIT, USA, **Vicenzo Consolo** Writer, Italy, **Jonathan Cook** Writer, Journalist, Israel, **Georges Corm** Writer, Former Minister of Finance, Lebanon, **Mairead Corrigan Maguire** Nobel Peace Prize 1976, Northern Ireland, **Miguel Angel Estrella** Pianist, Former Ambassador to UNESCO, Argentine, **Irene Fernandez** Right Livelihood Award 2005, Malaysia, **Norman Finkelstein** Writer, USA, **Cees Flinterman** Director of the Netherlands Institute of Human Rights, Netherlands, **Eduardo Galeano** Writer, Uruguay, **Johan Galtung** Founder and Co-director of Transcend, Right Livelihood Award 1987, Norway, **Geraud de Geouffre de la Pradelle** Professor Emeritus, France, **Juan Goytisolo** Writer, Spain, **Trevor Griffiths** Writer, UK, **Gisele Halimi** Lawyer, Former Ambassador to UNESCO, France, **Jeff Halper** Coordinator of the Israeli Committee Against House Demolitions, Israel, **Mohammed Harbi** Historian, Algeria, **Eric Hazan** Writer, France, **Stephane Hessel** Ambassador, France, **François Houtart** Professor Emeritus, Belgium, **Albert Jacquard** Professor, France, **Alain Joxe** Director of Studies at the EHESS, France, **Naomi Klein** Writer, USA, **Felicia Langer** Lawyer, Writer, Right Livelihood Award 1990, Germany, **Paul Laverty** Screenwriter, UK, **Ken Loach** Filmmaker, UK, **José Antonio Martin Pallin** Magistrado Emérito Sala II, Tribunal Supremo, Spain, **François Maspero** Writer, France, **Gustave Massiah** Chairman of CRID, France, **Avi Mograbi** Filmmaker, Israel, **Radhia Nasraoui** Human Rights Lawyer, Tunisia, **Susie Orbach** Professor, UK, **Simone Paris de Bollardière** Movement for Non-violence Alternative, France, **Tamar Pelleg-Sryck** Human Rights Lawyer, Israel, **Artur Pestana 'Pepetela'** Writer, Angola, **Jeremy Pikser** Writer, USA, **Harold Pinter** Writer, Nobel Prize for Literature 2005, UK, **François Rigaux** Professor Emeritus, Belgium, **Jacqueline Rose** Professor, UK, **Eric Rouleau**, Writer, Former Ambassador, France, **François Roux** Lawyer, France, **Jean Salmon** Professor Emeritus, ULB, Belgium, **Elias Sanbar** Writer, Palestine, **José Saramago** Nobel Prize for Literature 1998, Portugal, **Raji Surani** Vice-President of the FIDHs, Palestine, **Vandana Shiva** Right Livelihood Award 1993, India, **Sulak Sivaraksa** Professor, Right Livelihood Award 1995, Thailand, **Philippe Texier** Magistrate and Member of the UN Human Rights Committee, France, **Gerard Toulouse** Physician, France, **Andy de la Tour**

Actor/Screenwriter, UK, **Sir Brian Urquhart** Former Undersecretary-General of the United Nations, UK, **Itala Vivan** Professor, Italy, **Naomi Wallace** Playwright/Screenwriter, USA, **Michel Warschawski** Activist, Israel, **Francisco Whitaker** Right Livelihood Award 2006, Brazil, **Betty Williams** Nobel Peace Prize 1976, Northern Ireland, **Jody Williams** Nobel Peace Prize 1997, USA.

Call for contribution

The Russell Tribunal on Palestine aims to be a high quality moral, intellectual and scientific contribution, with the purpose of restoring rights and dignity to a people. It is open to any qualified person who feels they can contribute as expert, witness, assistant in the organisation of the Tribunal, or of a national support Committee. Essential financial support is welcome.

Organising Committee of the Tribunal

Ken Coates, Pierre Galand, Stéphane Hessel, Marcel-Francis Kahn, Robert Kissous, François Maspero, Paulette Pierson-Mathy, Bernard Ravenel, Brahim Senouci

Secretariat/information

Brussels, Forum Nord Sud, 115, rue Stévin, B, 1000 Brussels, Belgium,
Tel. fax + 32 (0)2 231 01 74
Paris, T.R.P. 21 ter Rue Voltaire 75011 Paris, France
England, Bertrand Russell Peace Foundation, Russell House, Bulwell Lane,
Nottingham NG6 0BT
Email, trp_int@yahoo.com
Bank account, IBAN: BE92 7330 3871 2023 // BIC: KREDBEBB

Footnote
1. Speech by Bertrand Russell to the First Meeting of Members of the War Crimes Tribunal, London, 13 November 1966 in *Autobiography* (Allen & Unwin, 1969) vol. III, pp 215.

OBAMA ON CUBA

Following our analysis of Senator Obama's Afghanistan policy in Spokesman 99, we publish his recent remarks about Cuba, and the response they drew from President Castro. These excerpts are taken from the Senator's address to the Cuban Independence Day Luncheon hosted by the Cuban American National Foundation in Miami, Florida, on 23 May 2008.

'... It's time for a new alliance of the Americas. After eight years of the failed policies of the past, we need new leadership for the future. After decades pressing for top-down reform, we need an agenda that advances democracy, security, and opportunity from the bottom up. So my policy towards the Americas will be guided by the simple principle that what's good for the people of the Americas is good for the United States. That means measuring success not just through agreements among governments, but also through the hopes of the child in the *favelas* of Rio, the security for the policeman in Mexico City, and the answered cries of political prisoners heard from jails in Havana.

The first and most fundamental freedom that we must work for is political freedom. The United States must be a relentless advocate for democracy.

I grew up for a time in Indonesia. It was a society struggling to achieve meaningful democracy. Power could be undisguised and indiscriminate. Too often, power wore a uniform, and was unaccountable to the people. Some still had good reason to fear a knock on the door.

There is no place for this kind of tyranny in this hemisphere. There is no place for any darkness that would shut out the light of liberty. Here we must heed the words of Dr. King, written from his own jail cell: 'Injustice anywhere is a threat to justice everywhere.'

Throughout my entire life, there has been injustice in Cuba. Never, in my lifetime, have the people of Cuba known freedom. Never, in the lives of two generations of Cubans, have the people of Cuba known democracy. This is the terrible and tragic status quo that we have known for half a century – of elections that are anything but free or fair; of dissidents locked away in dark prison cells for the crime of speaking the truth. I won't stand for this injustice, you won't stand for this injustice, and together we will stand up for freedom in Cuba.

Now I know what the easy thing is to do for American politicians. Every four years, they come down to Miami, they talk tough, they go back to Washington, and nothing changes in Cuba. That's what John McCain did the other day.

He joined the parade of politicians who make the same empty promises year after year, decade after decade. Instead of offering a strategy for change, he chose to distort my position, embrace George Bush's, and continue a policy that's done nothing to advance freedom for the Cuban people. That's the political posture that John McCain has chosen, and all it shows is that you can't take his so-called straight talk seriously.

My policy toward Cuba will be guided by one word: *Libertad*. And the road to freedom for all Cubans must begin with justice for Cuba's political prisoners, the rights of free speech, a free press and freedom of assembly; and it must lead to elections that are free and fair.

Now let me be clear. John McCain's been going around the country talking about how much I want to meet with Raul Castro, as if I'm looking for a social gathering. That's never what I've said, and John McCain knows it. After eight years of the disastrous policies of George Bush, it is time to pursue direct diplomacy, with friend and foe alike, without preconditions. There will be careful preparation. We will set a clear agenda. And as President, I would be willing to lead that diplomacy at a time and place of my choosing, but only when we have an opportunity to advance the interests of the United States, and to advance the cause of freedom for the Cuban people.

I will never, ever, compromise the cause of liberty. And unlike John McCain, I would never, ever, rule out a course of action that could advance the cause of liberty. We've heard enough empty promises from politicians like George Bush and John McCain. I will turn the page.

It's time for more than tough talk that never yields results. It's time for a new strategy. There are no better ambassadors for freedom than Cuban Americans. That's why I will immediately allow unlimited family travel and remittances to the island. It's time to let Cuban Americans see their mothers and fathers, their sisters and brothers.

It's time to let Cuban American money make their families less dependent upon the Castro regime.

I will maintain the embargo. It provides us with the leverage to present the regime with a clear choice: if you take significant steps toward democracy, beginning with the freeing of all political prisoners, we will take steps to begin normalising relations. That's the way to bring about real change in Cuba – through strong, smart and principled diplomacy.'

CASTRO ON OBAMA

President Castro listened to Senator Obama's remarks and, later the same day, wrote down his own reflections and some questions arising from what he had heard.

It would be dishonest of me to remain silent after hearing the speech Obama delivered on the afternoon of 23 May at the Cuban American National Foundation created by Ronald Reagan. I listened to his speech, as I did McCain's and Bush's. I feel no resentment towards him, for he is not responsible for the crimes perpetrated against Cuba and humanity. Were I to defend him, I would do his adversaries an enormous favour. I have therefore no reservations about criticising him and about expressing my points of view on his words frankly.

What were Obama's statements?

'Throughout my entire life, there has been injustice and repression in Cuba. Never, in my lifetime, have the people of Cuba known freedom. Never, in the lives of two generations of Cubans, have the people of Cuba known democracy. (…) This is the terrible and tragic status quo that we have known for half a century – of elections that are anything but free or fair (…) I won't stand for this injustice, you won't stand for this injustice, and together we will stand up for freedom in Cuba,' he told annexationists, adding: 'It's time to let Cuban American money make their families less dependent upon the Castro regime. (…) I will maintain the embargo.'

The content of these declarations by this strong candidate to the US presidency spares me the work of having to explain the reason for this reflection.

José Hernandez, one of the Cuban American National Foundation directors whom Obama praises in his speech, was none other than the owner of the 50-calibre automatic rifle, equipped with telescopic and infrared sights, which was confiscated, by chance, along with other deadly weapons while being transported by sea to Venezuela, where the Foundation had planned to assassinate the writer of these lines at an international meeting held in Margarita, in the Venezuelan state of Nueva Esparta.

Pepe Hernández' group wanted to renegotiate a former pact with Clinton, betrayed by Mas Canosa's clan, who secured Bush's electoral victory in 2000 through fraud, because the latter had promised to assassinate Castro, something they all happily embraced. These are the kinds of political tricks inherent to the United States' decadent and contradictory system.

Presidential candidate Obama's speech may be formulated as follows: hunger for the nation, remittances as charitable hand-outs, and visits to Cuba as propaganda for consumerism and the unsustainable way of life behind it.

How does he plan to address the extremely serious problem of the food crisis? The world's grains must be distributed among human beings, pets and fish, which become smaller every year and more scarce in the seas that have been over-exploited by the large trawlers which no international organization could get in the way of. Producing meat from gas and oil is no easy feat. Even Obama overestimates technology's potential in the fight against climate change, though he is more conscious of the risks and the limited margin of time than Bush. He could seek the advice of Gore, who is also a democrat and is no longer a candidate, as he is aware of the accelerated pace at which global warming is advancing. His close political rival Bill Clinton, who is not running for the presidency, an expert on extra-territorial laws like the Helms-Burton and Torricelli Acts, can advise him on an issue like the blockade, which he promised to lift and never did.

What did he say in his speech in Miami, this man who is doubtless, from the social and human points of view, the most progressive candidate for the US presidency?

'For two hundred years,' he said, 'the United States has made it clear that we won't stand for foreign intervention in our hemisphere. But every day, all across the Americas, there is a different kind of struggle – not against foreign armies, but against the deadly threat of hunger and thirst, disease and despair. That is not a future that we have to accept – not for the child in Port au Prince or the family in the highlands of Peru. We can do better. We must do better. (…) We cannot ignore suffering to our south, nor stand for the globalisation of the empty stomach.'

A magnificent description of imperialist globalisation: the globalisation of empty stomachs! We ought to thank him for it. But, 200 years ago, Bolivar fought for Latin American unity and, more than 100 years ago, Martí gave his life in the struggle against the annexation of Cuba by the United States. What is the difference between what Monroe proclaimed and what Obama proclaims and resuscitates in his speech two centuries later?

'I will reinstate a Special Envoy for the Americas in my White House who will work with my full support. But we'll also expand the Foreign Service, and open more consulates in the neglected regions of the Americas. We'll expand the Peace Corps, and ask more young Americans to go abroad to deepen the trust and the ties among our people,' he said near the end, adding: 'Together, we can choose the future over the past.'

A beautiful phrase, for it attests to the idea, or at least the fear, that history makes figures what they are and not the other way around.

Today, the United States has nothing of the spirit behind the Philadelphia declaration of principles formulated by the 13 colonies that rebelled against English colonialism. Today, they are a gigantic empire undreamed of by the country's founders at the time. Nothing, however, was to change for the natives and the slaves. The former were exterminated as the nation expanded; the latter continued to be auctioned at the marketplace – men, women and children – for nearly a century, despite the fact that 'all men are born free and equal', as the Declaration of Independence affirms. The world's objective conditions favoured the development of that system.

In his speech, Obama portrays the Cuban revolution as anti-democratic and lacking in respect for freedom and human rights. It is the exact same argument which, almost without exception, US administrations have used again and again to justify their crimes against our country. The blockade, in and of itself, is an act of genocide. I don't want to see US children inculcated with those shameful values.

An armed revolution in our country might not have been needed without the military interventions, Platt Amendment and economic colonialism visited upon Cuba.

The revolution was the result of imperial domination. We cannot be accused of having imposed it upon the country. The true changes could have and ought to have been brought about in the United States. Its own workers, more than a century ago, voiced the demand for an eight-hour work shift, which stemmed from the development of productive forces.

The first thing the leaders of the Cuban revolution learned from Martí was to believe in and act on behalf of an organisation founded for the purposes of bringing about a revolution. We were always bound by previous forms of power and, following the institutionalisation of this organisation, we were elected by more than 90 per cent of voters, as has become customary in Cuba, a process which does not in the least resemble the ridiculous levels of electoral participation which, many a time, as in the case of the United States, stay short of 50 per cent of the voters. No small and blockaded country like ours would have been able to hold its ground for so long on the basis of ambition, vanity, deceit or the abuse of power, the kind of power its neighbour has. To state otherwise is an insult to the intelligence of our heroic people.

I am not questioning Obama's great intelligence, his debating skills or his work ethic. He is a talented orator and is ahead of his rivals in the electoral race. I feel sympathy for his wife and little girls, who accompany him and give him encouragement every Tuesday. It is indeed a touching human spectacle. Nevertheless, I am obliged to raise a number of delicate questions. I do not expect answers; I wish only to raise them for the record.

1) Is it right for the president of the United States to order the assassination of any one person in the world, whatever the pretext may be?

2) Is it ethical for the president of the United States to order the torture of other human beings?

3) Should state terrorism be used by a country as powerful as the United States as an instrument to bring about peace on the planet?

4) Is an Adjustment Act, applied as punishment on only one country, Cuba, in order to destabilise it, good and honourable, even when it costs innocent children and mothers their lives? If it is good, why is this right not automatically granted to Haitians, Dominicans, and other peoples of the Caribbean, and why isn't the same Act applied to Mexicans and people from Central and South America, who die like flies against the Mexican border wall or in the waters of the Atlantic and the Pacific?

5) Can the United States do without immigrants, who grow vegetables, fruits, almonds and other delicacies for US citizens? Who would sweep their streets, work as servants in their homes, or do the worst and lowest-paid jobs?

6) Are crackdowns on illegal residents fair, even as they affect children born in the United States?

7) Are the brain-drain and the continuous theft of the best scientific and intellectual minds in poor countries moral and justifiable?

8) You state, as I pointed out at the beginning of this reflection, that your country had long ago warned European powers that it would not tolerate any intervention in the hemisphere, reiterating that this right be respected while demanding the right to intervene anywhere in the world with the aid of hundreds of military bases and naval, aerial and spatial forces distributed across the planet. I ask: is that the way in which the United States expresses its respect for freedom, democracy and human rights?

9) Is it fair to stage pre-emptive attacks on sixty or more dark corners of the world, as Bush calls them, whatever the pretext may be?

10) Is it honourable and sound to invest millions and millions of dollars in the military industrial complex, to produce weapons that can destroy life on earth several times over?

Before judging our country, you should know that Cuba, with its education, health, sports, culture and sciences programmes, implemented not only in its own territory but also in other poor countries around the world, and the blood that has been shed in acts of solidarity towards other peoples, in spite of the economic and financial blockade and the aggression of your powerful country, is proof that much can be done with very little. Not even our closest ally, the Soviet Union, was able to achieve what we have.

The only form of co-operation the United States can offer other nations consists in the sending of military professionals to those countries. It cannot offer anything else, for it lacks a sufficient number of people willing to sacrifice themselves for others and offer substantial aid to a country in need (though Cuba has known and relied on the co-operation of excellent US doctors). They are not to blame for this, for society does not inculcate such values in them on a massive scale.

We have never subordinated co-operation with other countries to ideological requirements. We offered the United States our help when hurricane Katrina lashed the city of New Orleans. Our internationalist medical brigade bears the glorious name of Henry Reeve, a young man, born in the United States, who fought and died for Cuba's sovereignty in our first war of independence.

Our revolution can mobilise tens of thousands of doctors and health technicians. It can mobilise an equally vast number of teachers and citizens, who are willing to travel to any corner of the world to fulfil any noble purpose, not to usurp people's rights or take possession of raw materials.

The goodwill and determination of people constitute limitless resources that cannot be kept and would not fit in a bank's vault. They cannot spring from the hypocritical politics of an empire.

WAR CRIMES IN DERRY

On 11 June 2008, six anti-war activists, who had occupied arms manufacturer Raytheon's offices in Derry and destroyed its computers during Israel's war on Lebanon in 2006, were found not guilty by a unanimous verdict of the jury in Belfast. After their acquittal on three charges of criminal damage to the computer equipment and office of Raytheon, the world's largest supplier of Guided Bomb Units, Colm Bryce and Eamonn McCann spoke to supporters and press outside the court. Colm Bryce began:

'The Raytheon 9 have been acquitted today in Belfast for their action in decommissioning the Raytheon offices in Derry in August 2006. The prosecution could produce not a shred of evidence to counter our case that we had acted to prevent the commission of war crimes during the Lebanon war by the Israeli armed forces using weapons supplied by Raytheon.

We remain proud of the action we took and only wish that we could have done more to disrupt the "kill chain" that Raytheon controls. This victory is welcome, for ourselves and our families, but we wish to dedicate it to the Shaloub and Hasheem families of Qana in Lebanon, who lost 28 of their closest relatives on the 30 July 2006 due to a Raytheon "bunker buster" bomb. Their unimaginable loss was foremost in our minds when we took the action we did on 9 August, and the injustice that they and the many thousands of victims of war crimes in Lebanon, Palestine, Iraq and Afghanistan have suffered, will spur us on to continue to campaign against war and the arms trade that profits from it.

We said from the beginning that we came to this court not as the accused but as the accusers of Raytheon. This court case proved that Raytheon in Derry is an integral part of the global Raytheon company and its military production. This is no longer a secret or in doubt. Raytheon have treated the truth, peaceful protest, local democracy and this court with complete contempt. The most senior executive who appeared said that the charge that Raytheon had "aided and abetted" the commission of crimes against humanity was "not an issue" for him. Raytheon should have that contempt repaid in full and be driven out of Derry and every other place they have settled. They are war criminals, plain and simple. They have no place in our society and shame on all those in positions of power or influence who would hand them public funds, turn a blind eye to their crimes, cover their tracks or make excuses for them ...

We feel totally vindicated by this decision and wish to extend our heartfelt thanks to all of those who gave us support ... we particularly want to thank the jury who listened intently through three weeks of evidence before ensuring that justice was done today.'

Eamonn McCann then addressed supporters and press saying:

'The outcome of this case has profound implications. The jury has accepted that we were reasonable in our belief that the Israel Defence Forces were guilty of war crimes in Lebanon in the summer of 2006; that the Raytheon company, including its facility in Derry, was aiding and abetting the commission of these crimes; and that the action we took was intended to have, and did have, the effect of hampering or delaying the commission of war crimes.

We have been vindicated. We reject entirely and with contempt the statement by Raytheon this evening suggesting that the result of the trial gives them concern about the safety of their employees. This is an abject attempt to divert attention from the significance of the outcome. Not a shred of evidence was produced that we presented the slightest danger to Raytheon workers. The charge of affray was thrown out by the court without waiting to hear defence evidence.

Our target has always been Raytheon as a corporate entity and its shareholders and directors who profit from misery and death. There is now no hiding place for those who have said that they support the presence of Raytheon in Derry on the basis that the company is not involved in Derry in arms-related production. We have established that not only is the Derry plant involved in arms-related production, it is also, through its integration into Raytheon as a whole, involved in war crimes. We call on all elected representatives in Derry, and on the citizens of Derry, to say now in unequivocal terms that the war criminal Raytheon is not welcome in our city.

We call on the office of the Attorney General and the Crown Prosecution Service, in light of this verdict, to institute an investigation into the activities of Raytheon at its various plants across the UK, with a view to determining whether Raytheon is, as we say it is, a criminal enterprise.

We believe that one day the world will look back on the arms trade as we look back today on the slave trade, and wonder how it came about that such evil could abound in respectable society. If we have advanced by a mere moment the day when the arms trade is put beyond the law, what we have done will have been worthwhile.

We took the action we did in the immediate aftermath of the slaughter of innocents in Qana on July 30th 2006. The people of Qana are our neighbours. Their children are the children of our neighbours. We trashed Raytheon to help protect our neighbours. The court has found that that was not a crime. This what the Raytheon case has been about.

We have not denied or apologised for what we did at the Raytheon plant in the summer of 2006. All of us believe that it was the best thing we ever did in our lives.'

source:www.raytheon9.org

unite
the**UNION**

London & Eastern Region
Woodberry
218 Green Lanes
London
N4 2HB

Marking 50 years of CND

Let's work to ensure that we do not have to wait another 50 years to free the world of the madness of nuclear weapons

On this anniversary, we remember with pride the work of our former Regional Secretary, Ron Todd

Steve Hart   *Regional Secretary*

020.8800.4281   www.unitetheunion.com

Bakers, Food & Allied Workers Union

Supporting workers in struggle
Wherever they may be.

Joe Marino   General Secretary
Ronnie Draper   President
Jackie Barnwell Vice President

Stanborough House,
Great North Road,
Stanborough,
Welwyn Garden City,
Hertfordshire. AL8 7TA

Phone 01707 260150 & 01707 259450
www.bfawu.org

Reviews

Cuba Crisis

Len Scott, *The Cuban Missile Crisis and the Threat of Nuclear War – Lessons from History,* Continuum Publishing, 222 pages, hardback ISBN 9781847060266, £25

This book is perfectly described by its title. The events of those critical days of October 1962 for the whole world are set out in impressive detail. Most of us have seen similar accounts written by top-level contemporary participants, but memoirs understandably tend to show their authors in the best light. Len Scott has given us a record of events which is more detached.

The Cuba crisis was the highest of high-wire balancing acts. Both superpowers were equipped with massive nuclear weapon arsenals. Had a small proportion of the total exploded anywhere, life on earth as we know it would have ground to an end. George Kennan, one of the architects of the Cold War, described, in his later years, the level of weaponry as 'grotesque'. It was to grow even more grotesque in the Reagan years during an arms race which led, as intended, to the financial ruin of the Soviet Union.

But 'Lessons from History' ? They are there to be learnt but we do not learn them. Nikita Khrushchev wrote these words to President Kennedy on 26 October, at the height of the crisis,

> 'If people do not show wisdom then in the final analysis they will come to a clash like blind moles and then reciprocal extermination will begin'.

It very nearly did. Blind moles is an appropriate metaphor. What the book makes clear is that often enough neither side knew what the other side meant or intended. Communication travelled by unusual channels. Participants put their own glosses on messages. Assumptions were made of the most dangerous kind. For instance, members of the US Executive Committee of the National Security Council thought that Moscow could communicate with its nuclear weapon-armed submarines. But that meant the submarines coming to the surface. Submarine captains underwater were indeed blind moles.

The account of what went on in one such submarine is enough to show how extreme were the levels of risk. Captain Valentin Savitsky was in charge of one. For four hours during the blockade they had been submerged underneath United States warships which were trying to get them to surface by dropping small explosives – not of depth charge size. Temperatures had risen to 60 degrees centigrade. Crew members were collapsing under the strain and heat. Savitsky ordered the officer responsible for the nuclear torpedoes to assemble one at battle readiness. He is quoted as saying,

> 'Maybe the war has already started up there while we are doing somersaults here … we are going to blast them now. We will die but we will sink them all. We will not disgrace our navy.'

Fortunately, even at such a time of tension, wiser words prevailed. The submarine came up to the surface.

What would have happened had a nuclear torpedo been fired? Who knows. The book is full of hypotheticals. What if this? What if that? What if the other? It may well have been that, in the eventuality of an actual firing of one, or a few, nuclear weapons 'the other side' may have realised that full-scale war was not intended. Perhaps a junior officer had exceeded his duties. Perhaps there had been an accident. Whatever the hypotheticals, the dangers were very great indeed. One can play poker with limited stakes without any worry. But this, as the author makes clear, was not poker and the stakes were not limited.

There were other critical moments. It was not just a matter of one submarine captain getting hysterical. A U2 was shot down over Cuba and the US hawks wanted retaliation. Fortunately, Kennedy had taken direct control himself, and the powers of the hawks were limited. Another U2 went into Soviet air space as if reconnoitring for a nuclear first strike. The Soviets did not respond as they might have done. A taped simulation of a Soviet attack was put into a computer and for a short time it seemed that an American city had been targeted. Kennedy did not panic.

Robert McNamara said when he came over to England recently: 'we were saved not by good judgement but by good luck'. Nuclear deterrence presupposes extreme rationality and accident free procedures.

This most interesting book is another reminder of what the report of the first United Nations Special Session on Disarmament said in 1978:

> 'Enduring international peace and security cannot be built on the accumulation of weaponry by military alliances nor be sustained by a precarious balance of deterrence or doctrines of strategic superiority'.

If there is a weakness in the book it lies in the author's own apparent lack of knowledge about current nuclear disarmament opportunities. He asks, in his last chapter, this important question: what will it take 'to create the political conditions for nuclear disarmament?' One should not ask questions of such importance and not try to answer them.

I commend to him the draft abolition treaty prepared by the International Campaign to Abolish Nuclear Weapons (ICAN) and lodged with the United Nations by Costa Rica. As global opinion begins to understand that nuclear weapons do nothing to solve the actual problems of insecurity today, the political conditions are moving in a more rational direction.

Bruce Kent

Saskatchewan Uranium

Jim Harding, *Canada's Deadly Secret: Saskatchewan Uranium and the Global Nuclear System,* Fernwood Publishing (Ocean Vista Lane, Black Point, Nova Scotia BOJ 1BO, Canada) 272 pages, paperback ISBN 9781552662267, £13.95

Jim Harding, the author of this detailed account of Saskatchewan's engagement with the nuclear industry, is a retired Professor of Environment and Justice Studies. Like the sociologist Charles Perrow, who wrote *Normal Accidents,* he has learned several new disciplines as a persistent inquirer into the nuclear business and he rewards his readers with plenty of little-published but well-validated information. His message in brief is that there is no peaceful atom, no safe radioactive waste management, and many health hazards.

Because of Canada's rich sources of uranium ore in the north of the province of Saskatchewan, Harding starts with mining – the front end of the nuclear business. We learn that the inhabitants discovered later that, from 1953 to 1969, all the uranium mined in Saskatchewan went to make the massive stockpile of US nuclear weapons. Mine sites remain largely un-restored, with waste in the form of tailings – finely-divided, crushed rock in mine tips or in semi-liquid suspension in lagoons – left behind to pollute the land, air and water supplies and the food chain of the people who live there. These radioactive residues, often uncharted, amount to millions of tons and worldwide to hundreds of millions of tons. In the USA a total of 250 million tons has been estimated, and in Canada close to 200 million tons.

In the United Kingdom, since the Aberfan tip slide which included tailings and which killed 144 people in October 1966, 112 of them children, we have legislation on tips and lagoons. The Mines and Quarries (Tips) Act 1969 and its regulations require design by qualified persons, site surveys, geotechnical assessment, tip design specifications, and competent supervision and inspection. Such regulation is not found worldwide. At a recent meeting of the Institution of Mining Engineers in Cardiff we heard that tailings dams have been built up to 100m high and that, worldwide, tailings dam failures still occur at a reported rate of 25 a year. The explanation for such hubris in design is that neither governments abroad nor investors have seen fit to set constraints. The difference between a 'successful' design and a similar one that failed can be little more than that one was affected by landslip causing overtopping or by earth tremors sufficient to cause solids to behave as liquids.

Jim Harding describes lagoon failures resulting in the release of millions of litres of radioactive liquid. Because Canada was a founding partner of the Manhattan project to produce atomic bombs, it is not surprising that radiation hazards were not acknowledged or they were understated. Even as late as 1989, the Canada Nuclear Association, in a pamphlet, *How Do We Protect the Environment in Uranium Mining,* used in schools, failed to state that uranium tailings are radioactive. Thorium, for example, has a half life of 76,000 years and for one and a half million years will continue to generate carcinogenic radon daughters. Not only mine workers have been affected. By 1990, it was reported that 300 miners in Ontario had died of lung cancer – likely to have been caused by the inhalation and ingestion of radon daughter particles. Pollution on the scale described means that local communities also are vulnerable to polluted air, water and food. Many of the local communities are indigenous Americans whose concerns about land rights are not yet alleviated.

In the period reviewed by Jim Harding, permitted levels of occupational exposure to ionising radiation were reduced from 350 millisieverts per year (350mSv) to 50mSv per year and, by 1990, the International Commission on Radiological Protection advised a maximum dose of 20mSv per year averaged over five years. Now it is accepted by the US National Academy of Sciences Committee on the Biological Effects of Ionising Radiation (BEIR) that there is no safe level of exposure, and in the United Kingdom we require operators to limit exposure to members of the public to 1mSv per year. There was consternation when experts advised Sellafield workers to think twice about having children, but it remains pertinent for us to think of the reasons that allow people in industry to be exposed to doses 50 times higher than those permitted to members of the public. Harding reports that traces of depleted uranium have been detected in air in Britain which can be correlated with the use of depleted uranium weapons by coalition forces in Iraq. Such controversy as remains in dose assessments appears to lie between the International Atomic Energy Agency, whose mandate is to promote the use of atomic energy, and the World Health Organisation, which appears to have a subordinate role in matters nuclear. Perhaps we should be hearing much more from the WHO on world trends in the incidence of radiation related diseases such as leukaemia and myeloma.

The political climate in which the nuclear industry developed in Canada is examined with the author's particular interest, and sometimes dismay, in the positions taken by the New Democratic Party (NDP). In 1963, the NDP opposed the placing of US nuclear armed missiles on Canadian soil but, by 1971, the Saskatchewan NDP provincial government was seeking a uranium enrichment plant and, in 1973, unsuccessfully sought a heavy water plant. In 1974, the NDP provincial government created the public uranium corporation Saskatchewan Mining and Development Corporation (SMDC). This was the climate in which Atomic Energy of Canada Ltd sought to sell its Candu reactor to Argentina's military government, and came close to selling one to Iraq. In 1979, the NDP provincial government formed the Uranium Secretariat whose publications were regarded by the no-nuclear movement as disinformation and, in that year, the Regina Group for Non-Nuclear Society published Jim Harding's father's anti-nuclear *Correspondence with the Premier.*

In 1981, with Ronald Reagan in the White House escalating a second nuclear arms race, the demand for uranium increased and US cruise missile testing began in western Canada. In 1987, some months after the Chernobyl explosion, the Inter-

Church Uranium Committee (ICUC) was campaigning to make Saskatoon a nuclear-weapons-free zone. As in Europe, the debate between the advocates of a nuclear and a non-nuclear society was in full swing. Jim Harding records instances of bias – in official enquiries such as those into nuclear spills, in the regulators' promotion of the industry, and in the industry's so-called educational material. He reports the not-so-readily acknowledged public subsidy of £500bn for the nuclear industry in the USA and describes the insurance waivers and other subsidies which provided the appearance of viability for a Canadian industry that could not manage its waste and which made inadequate provision for an already polluted future. The neglect of developments in renewable energy, and the insupportable claims that new nuclear reactors could have a timely effect on climate change, are the topics of the final chapters of the book.

This is a book that comes closer than many others to exploring the reasons for institutional support for all matters nuclear in the face of the world-wide proliferation of nuclear weapon-making material and the radiation hazards now enlarged by the threat of terrorism. In the United Kingdom terrorism is a topic that the government and the regulators now refuse to discuss on the grounds of national security, in spite of their statutory duty to provide information to the public[1].

One has to conclude that mendacity in matters nuclear is international. Two recent examples in the United Kingdom must be mentioned. Our government's last two consultations on its already-taken decision to encourage the building of new nuclear reactors were invalid for that reason. A High Court judge described the first as 'misleading and unlawful'. On waste management the government modified the conclusions of its waste management committee (CoRWM) to claim that co-disposal of legacy waste and waste from new build was feasible. (Did you know that the difference between a repository and a depository has been abolished by the government's definition of the one being the same as the other?)[2]

Researchers have since argued that co-disposal of the hotter higher activity spent fuel waste will require a repository three times larger than one for legacy waste alone.

The conclusion reached by Hugh Richards, an anti-nuclear campaigning colleague, in *Too Hot to Handle*[3], that no feasible design of such a repository exists is supported by the far from dove-like International Atomic Energy Agency. Last year they warned that Britain must not go ahead with a new generation of nuclear power stations until it has a 'clear and robust' plan in place for dealing with the twin problems of decommissioning and waste treatment. The agency's executive director said:

'The spent fuel issue is the most critical one for nuclear. It will not develop if there is not a credible and satisfactory answer to the management of spent fuel and one that is convincing for the public. '

No such facility exists here or anywhere else. This is reminiscent of the 1976 but still extant recommendation of the Sixth Report of the Royal Commission on Environmental Pollution[4] which stated that there should be no commitment to a large nuclear power programme 'until it has been established beyond reasonable doubt that a method exists to ensure the safe containment of long lived highly radioactive waste for the indefinite future'. Of the 'indefinite future' the Commission said

> 'We must assume that these wastes will remain dangerous and will need to be isolated from the biosphere for hundreds of thousands of years. In considering arrangements for dealing with such waste man is faced with time scales that transcend his experience.'

We are left to ponder what experience and disposition makes for hawks and doves in the nuclear debate. Jim Harding makes the connection throughout that you start with the bomb. If you can contemplate the death of a million people at the push of a button you are on the way to being a reactor hawk. There are few who would be without the bomb but still want a reactor and all its problems.

The book has a chronology of Canadian nuclear affairs but would benefit also from an index. A foreword by Helen Caldicott, whose most recent book *Nuclear Power is Not the Answer* was reviewed in *Spokesman 99*, sets the scene and supports the author in his conclusions.

Christopher Gifford

Footnotes

1 The regulations dealing with foreseeable emergencies are the Radiation (Emergency Preparedness and Public Information) Regulations 2001 SI: 2971.

2 In *Managing Radioactive Waste Safely* DEFRA, DE and DTI 2007 page 67.

3 *Too Hot to Handle,* Hugh Richards 2008 – a response to the Welsh Assembly Government consultation on radioactive waste management.

4 In *Nuclear Power and the Environment* (also known as the Flowers report) Cmnd 618 HMSO 1976.

Hiding the Truth

Achin Vanaik (editor), *Selling US Wars*, 400 pages, Interlink Publishing/Transnational Institute, paperback ISBN 9781566566681, US$20

This collection of essays prepared by members of the Transnational Institute has been published at a particularly appropriate moment for those with an interest in North-South politics. Not that we haven't been here before. The United States bogged down in a war started on the pretext of a lie; oil prices going through the roof; the dollar collapsing. And add to these an asset bubble that is deflating in instalments as central banks, sometimes unilaterally, other times multilaterally, step in to nationalise tranches of their trading banks' debts, although all the while denying that is in fact what they're doing.

Achin Vanaik's introduction sets out the route that the discourse is to follow. The chosen starting point is the end of the Cold War and the collapse of communism. After the collapse of the Iron Curtain, it quickly became apparent that the use of the threat from the East, although useful in controlling radical movements in the West, revealed that the securitocracy of the West had been inhibited to the extent in which it wanted to control its own population and in how they wished to transfer economic control from state to private hands. Freed from these bounds, the United States in particular has set out to, as they would call it, 'expand freedom': much in the way that expanding freedom for the pike increases the possibility of death for the minnow.

Selling US Wars is mainly an investigation of the way in which the US attempts to manufacture consent for its actions. It has three spheres of influence in which to pedal its ideas: first, its own domestic audience, second, the target states, and, thirdly, the rest of the world. The book investigates US public diplomacy under six different 'ideological banners', or, for the sake of clarity, excuses. First is the 'global war on terror', then 'weapons of mass destruction', in the wrong hands of course, followed by 'failed states', 'humanitarian intervention', 'regime change in the name of democracy' and 'the war on drugs'.

Each of the chapters on these six themes are broadly united by their common concern (a) to identify the origins or emergence of the particular legitimizing discourse or ideological banner; (b) to examine the character and composition of the banner; (c) to point out the purposes or aims that lie behind the unfolding of the banner; (d) to evaluate how effective the use of the banner has actually been; (e) to highlight the falsity of the banner or the dishonesties, deceits, and hypocrisies that have guided or lain behind its use; (f) to suggest how in all moral honesty and seriousness one should address the particular problem, be it terrorism, violations of universal human rights, the proliferation of weapons of mass destruction, or opium, heroin, and cocaine production, distribution, and use.

Walden Bello's conclusion to his own contribution follows closely Tariq Ali's foreword quotation from Trotsky at the time of the Wall Street Crash, that the US will operate more ruthlessly under economic stress than during a period of boom. Bello's conclusion was written before the sub-prime market crash, so his comments about an economy built on easy credit awaiting their day of reckoning show some prescience.

The themes chosen and dissected are indeed powerful ones in the march from Cold War to neoliberal globalisation. The issues of American exceptionalism with regards to international law, and the shameful me-too antics of the United Kingdom government to provide legitimising cover for the US attempts to denigrate the UN, are well covered by Mariano Aguirre. He explores the use of the cover of humanitarian intervention to send in the military, which carries with it the useful collateral damage of fomenting splits in liberal ranks. All humanitarian intervention since and including the war on Yugoslavia has been carried out by military forces and, although ordered to the areas for relief by politicians, these forces have in their operations been directed by military logic. The skies have darkened with B-52 bombers flying overhead long before aid trucks and ambulances have been ordered in on the ground.

The appearance of Nato out of area, or wherever the US wishes to deploy, has changed the organisation's *raison d'être* from Cold War defence to power projection on behalf of the rich, white north against those of the poor black south who happen to be living on top of raw materials that the north requires. Why else would Britain have ordered two huge new aircraft carriers, except for future imperial interventions? It is worth pointing to the contribution of Phyllis Bennis and her comments on the effects of the great American adventure in Iraq on the extension of democracy in that wretched country:

'The reality in Iraq is (1) the establishment of an American puppet regime that will enable the US to have permanent military bases; (2) the shameful imposition of a basically American-drafted constitution under foreign occupation; (3) the promotion of a corporate privatization that most suits American business and state interests; (4) the activation of a divide-and-rule policy that has created terrible sectarian hostilities now threatening to become an enduring civil war. So much then for the US claim to promote democracy!'

The history of Britain's imperial past should have cautioned us against all of these problems, but it was our misfortune at this juncture to have the least informed Prime Minister with regards to foreign affairs in living memory. No one has been able to find any coherent foreign policy utterances traceable to Tony Blair prior to his elevation as Prime Minister. Under these circumstances, one would have thought that he might have at least shown some humility or perhaps have read the works of those with knowledge to offer on the subject. Perhaps he could start now by reading *Selling US Wars*, then enter a complete confession of guilt and a period of condign penance for all of the misery and suffering he has caused.

Henry McCubbin

Darwin's Legacy

Janet Browne, *Darwin's Origin of Species: A Biography,* 192 pages, Atlantic Books, ISBN 9781843543947, £7.99

In the year of the 200th anniversary of Charles Darwin's birth and the 150th of the publication of *Origin of Species*, which are to be celebrated at Cambridge in July 2009 (for programme see http//www. Darwin2009.cam.uk) there will be much spoken and written about the great man, and his influence ever since, on our ideas about evolution. A first start has already been made by Janet Browne, Darwin's foremost biographer, in a short and highly readable new biography. This covers the five year voyage of the *Beagle* (1831-36), Darwin' s studies of his immense collection of plants and bones, his long search for 'a theory with which to work', the publication of *Origin of Species* in 1859, the controversies which it aroused among scientists and churchmen, and, finally, the legacy which informs our present understanding of evolution.

Janet Browne devotes much attention to the influence on Darwin's thought of

Thomas Robert Malthus, whose book *An Essay on the Principle of Population* came into Darwin's hands in 1838. Although the book had been published forty years earlier, its thesis, that populations grow faster than the food supply to feed them, had received much attention during the 1830s food riots in Britain, when food prices rose as supplies dwindled, and protest grew about the protectionist Corn Laws and the repressive Poor Laws. The idea that the healthy and well fed survived while the poor and weak went to the wall seemed to be quite acceptable to those who were well placed. Farmers selected the herds and crops that had proved strongest. There was no divine intervention there, as those with religious beliefs saw in human history. 'But what happened in nature?', Darwin asked.

> 'Being well prepared to appreciate the struggle for existence,' he wrote in his *Autobiography*, 'it at once struck me that under these circumstances favourable variations would tend to be preserved, and unfavourable ones to be destroyed. Here then I had at last a theory by which to work'.

In fact it was Herbert Spencer who coined the phrase 'the survival of the fittest', and though Darwin came to use it, he was anxious to avoid any religious assumption of a divinely select people or the racist implications that came to be associated in Social Darwinism. Darwin wrote of 'natural selection', but later decided that a more neutral wording would have been more appropriate, such as 'natural preservation'. There should be no suggestion of an outside intelligence making the selection. It was the principle of divergence in development that Darwin insisted on. It was always advantageous for living beings to diversify. Those diversities best adapted to their surroundings survived, the others died out. This was how evolution took place over millions of years. This was, of course, what distanced him not only from the fundamentalists who believed that God created the earth and all that was on it, a few thousand years earlier, but also from those who saw subsequent changes as the intervention of a divine power or, in today's thought, of 'intelligent design'.

Controversy over Darwin's ideas raged most powerfully among those who sought to apply them to human development in the espousal, by many professional people, of the concept of eugenics, and the founding, in 1907, of an Eugenics Society, under the chairmanship of Darwin's son, Leonard. This had the explicit aim of 'improving and controlling the masses', in effect by sterilising those of supposedly low intelligence. Such 'Social Darwinism' was employed to justify slavery and colonial rule over 'lesser races without the law'. This had no support in scientific evidence.

Janet Browne's final chapter on the Legacy of Darwinism covers the discovery of genes and the reconciliation of Darwin's original proposals with the science of genetics, leading to Richard Dawkins' concept of the 'selfish gene', not meaning a gene for selfishness or for any other human characteristic, but a gene demanding its reproduction. Debates over these ideas provided an opening for a surprising revival of creationist thought, reaching even into school textbooks first in the United States and then in Britain.

What is perhaps unexpected is that Janet Browne says little or nothing about the influence of ideas of the survival of the fittest on economic theories. She recognises that Darwinian ideas took off at the end of the Nineteenth Century because they justified an economic system which rewarded the well placed in a fiercely competitive market. But she does not examine how the system works today.

The revolt in the 1930s, led by John Maynard Keynes, against *laissez-faire* in economic organisation was aimed deliberately at such competitive assumptions. But they have remained remarkably strong. Even a recent so-called 'New Labour' government in the United Kingdom has hesitated to intervene in the struggle for survival of workers, companies, and even banks, in a fiercely competitive market. The assumption that the fittest survive depends on the definition of fitness. It has to be asked what the competitors are fit for. They may be the fittest for making money, but the results of such competition are obviously not the best for human survival, even for the planet's survival, given the uncontrolled using up of resources, and the resultant destruction of the planet's self-generating capacities. Darwin was well aware that human survival, like the survival of many animals, depended on the evolution of a capacity to co-operate as well as to compete. He knew that Adam Smith, whose recommendations of competition are still enshrined in the promulgations of the Adam Smith Institute, advanced also the theory of moral sentiment. Without such safeguards, who indeed will survive?

Michael Barratt Brown

Ford and After

Huw Beynon and Theo Nichols (editors), *The Fordism of Ford and Modern Management: Fordism and Post-Fordism,* **Edward Elgar Publishing, two volume set, 1,032 pages, hardback ISBN 9781858989488, £295**
Huw Beynon and Theo Nichols (editors), *Patterns of Work in the Post-Fordist Era: Fordism and Post-Fordism,* **Edward Elgar Publishing, two volume set, 1,176 pages, hardback ISBN 9781845423247, £295, Elgar Reference Collection**

These two ponderous collections have brought together a variety of treatments of what Ethan Kapstein, the Director of Studies at the Council of Foreign Relations in New York, described as the break in the post-war bargain built around the Bretton Woods agreement.

'The global economy is leaving millions of disaffected workers in its train. Inequality, unemployment, and endemic poverty have become its handmaidens. Rapid technological change, and heightening international competition are fraying the job markets of the major industrialist countries. At the same time systemic pressures are curtailing every government's ability to respond with new spending. Just when working people need the nation state as a buffer from the world economy, it is abandoning them.'

The first two volumes of this collection give us an overview of industrial life according to Henry Ford, with an extensive excursion into the mores of the Japanese automobile industry. Innovation raced ahead, and the literature followed it in the 1980s, with extensive discussions of flexible specialisation and lean production, dissected in the second two volumes.

The shaping hand of the Marxist journal *Capital and Class* focuses our attention on what is called the Third Italy, and what is called 'the decline of the mass-collective worker'. The Third Italy bases itself on the analysis of small engineering firms in Emilia-Romagna, extending to the Marches, Tuscany and Umbria. In happier days, this wide region was known as the 'red belt', before the remorseless advance of the Italian Right. Its working practices represented the powerful continuity of an artisanal culture, suddenly revivified by the crisis of profitability in conventional industries. It had become necessary to find ways of intensifying productivity, if possible engaging a workforce whose alienation had become legendary, just as Ethan Kapstein was to report.

Much of the evidence for his dispiriting conclusion is drawn from journals with a socialist provenance: *Marxism Today* contributes pieces by John Atkinson and Denis Gregory, and by Doreen Massey. *Capital and Class* furnishes pieces by Bob Carter and Adam Tickell, and by John Holloway on conditions in Nissan. Another piece on call centres is gathered from *Soundings*. So many of our readers may already be familiar with some of these contributions.

How far is post-Fordism different from what went before? Possibly, it may be more profitable, more labour intensive, and more 'efficient'. But the numerous apologists who have celebrated its greater humanity will find a powerful indictment in these pages, which are anything but rosy in their appreciation of the meaning of these changes. Was it not Tolstoy who said that the masters would do anything for their serfs except get off their backs?

The book is structured into sections about the general meaning of Fordism and post-Fordism, the arguments about work organisation, skilling and deskilling, and then an important section on changes in the motor industry which examines changes in the Ford Motor Company and specific examples taken from Australia and Mexico, together with a case study of changes at Volkswagen in Brazil.

Another section looks at the applications of post-Fordist technologies outside the motor industry in other sectors including clothing, the broiler industry, and meat packing. Two sections consider the developments in call centres, and in financial services; one gives five case studies on customer services, and another considers employment in the State sector.

There is one study of developments in a privatised furniture company in Siberia, which emphasises a prevalent disillusionment among the workers. This gives rise to a serious gap in the work, which is in many respects very wide-ranging and catholic in its coverage. But nowhere does it examine any of the tumultuous events in China, where the mutations of capitalism have been extreme, and the implications of its experience convoluted.

Elizabeth Trapp

Exploration

Mike Marqusee, *If I Am Not for Myself: Journey of an Anti-Zionist Jew*, Verso, 320 pages, hardback ISBN 9781844672141, £16.99

Mike Marqusee will be familiar to readers of *The Spokesman* as an active political participant in the Left and anti-war movements in Britain, but also as a perceptive writer and journalist whose breadth of subject-matter encompasses cricket, the Labour Party and Bob Dylan. This latest offering is clearly a most personal and deeply-felt exploration of the connections between family, Jewishness, nationalism, Zionism and its wrongs. It is a brave endeavour, which places him firmly amongst the list of Jewish detractors from Zionism, along with such notables as Chomsky, Finkelstein, Barenboim, Pinter and others.

Predominantly, the substance of the book is negotiated through the life and vicissitudes of the author's maternal grandfather, Edward Vivien Morand, or EVM for short, and the discovery by Marqusee of an old luggage case containing his grandfather's papers. Morand, who added the 'd' to be more Jewish, was of Jewish Lithuanian stock on his maternal side with an Irish father who died shortly after his birth. Needless to say, EVM was quite a character: lawyer, radio broadcaster, aspiring congressman, journalist, political and community leader, trade unionist and, sadly, Zionist. EVM lived and worked in the Bronx all his life amongst the heterogeneous Jewish and Irish communities which dominated that area of New York up until the 1960s. His most active political period covered the 1930s till the late 1950s – the era of the Popular Front, the Nazi-Soviet Pact, the Second World War and its McCarthyite aftermath. This was a time fraught with apprehension for the Jews of the Bronx, a period well captured by the novel *The Plot against America* by Philip Roth. Although overt anti-Semitism is not the predominant form adopted by American racism, it was by no means uncommon well into the 1950s, with its undertones playing a part in McCarthyism. Racism's most common manifestation, of course, was reserved for those with a black skin, whose struggle EVM spent a lifetime supporting, as late as 1965 joining with Martin Luther King on the Selma march. There were, it seems, few struggles of the time that EVM was not involved in, from the Scottsboro boys, Sacco and Vanzetti, defence of the Spanish republic, anti-Nazi boycotts, and numerous activities within the Jewish community relating to Zionism. There is even a connection with Bertrand Russell and the New York 'Free Speech' campaign, formed initially over the cancellation of Russell's tenure at City College, which was driven by Christian clerics and politicians already distinguished in the service of anti-Semitism. Russell's victimisation was the beginning of a calculated campaign to restrict academic freedom and other lecturers were singled out for dismissal.

The book describes the political journey and travails of EVM through the mire of New York's Tammany Hall politics, the New Deal Democratic Party, the American Labour Party, the Socialist and Communist parties, and the unsuccessful candidature for President of Henry Wallace in 1948 for the ALP.

There is a great deal of insightful and informative writing about both the international and specifically American political scene in this period and its relevance to the subsequent evolution and stultifying of possible options for the American Left. With the end of the Second World War and the exposure of the full truth, in all its horror, of the fate of European Jewry, we see EVM move up a gear to defend the Palestine partition and the inchoate Israeli state, and failing to appreciate the terrible wrong being done to the Palestinian people. It was not a mistake that his grandson was to make.

The areas covered by the book are spread widely but connected in some way: Jewish history, philosophy, Zionism, Judaism and scripture which amply demonstrate Marqusee's intellectual prowess and commitment to a socialism defined by its humanism. It also covers issues related to the *Nakba*, the partition, British imperial policy towards Palestine, and the effects of the founding of Israel on the Jewish Diaspora in Arab lands, These insights on Jewish history, debates, schisms and ideas enable him to see parallels with other demonised communities, specifically the Islamic community in Western society. The obvious parallel is the many xenophobic attitudes common in the host societies: the idea of the secret agenda, the world conspiracy, the Elders of Zion, and the Al Qaeda caliphate, the supposed loyalty to a theological creed, Judaism and Islam. Marqusee sees the debates within the two communities as comparable also: should they pursue assimilation or separate development? Who are the community leaders and representatives to be: the synagogue and the mosque, or others? Much of Jewish history has been a battle against authority within the community and against religious conformity. Marqusee tells of visits and conversations about Jewish and Muslim identities and beliefs in the Asian sub-continent, but I expect they talked about cricket as well!

There are a small number of autobiographical vignettes throughout the book of which perhaps the most revealing is that of his adolescent experiences, growing up in suburban America. The young Marqusee, brought up within a family comfortably affluent, now matured from its tentative communist background to the liberal wing of Reformed Judaism, attending Sunday School to be taught scripture and the necessity to defend Israel and 'intoxicated by the ideas of justice and equality', discovers an inconsistency that troubles him profoundly. He attends a lecture at Sunday School class delivered by a soldier from the Israeli Defence Force fresh from victory in the Six Day War, who in the course of his peroration describes the native Palestinian population in terms akin to the racial slurs delivered by southern segregationists about Negroes, which of course he was familiar with. The youthful Marqusee questions this in both the lecture and at home and earns the censure of all, his father remarking that his son was suffering 'some Jewish self-hatred', a malady the luckless patient did not realise he had contracted. Further shocks are admonished at a Boy Scout camping holiday, where he meets for the first time overt anti-Semitism, at the end of which no doubt he felt distinctly less like one of 'the most comfortable Jews that ever walked the planet', a previous description by the author of modern American Jewry.

The book as a whole gives an insight into the processes by which the Jewish community within America, which had been in many ways like EVM a stalwart of Leftist movements in general, was ostensibly funnelled by Zionism and the reaction to the Holocaust into the slavish and vociferous support for the Israeli state, ignoring actions that they would not countenance closer to home. The importance to Israel of this support within the United States of the 'Jewish lobby', (Marqusee objects strongly to the term for reasons explained in the book, but basically, the portrayal of a non-existent uniformity of opinion within the Jewish community in support of Zionism) is important but by no means the deciding factor for the State Department's close relationship with Israel. He has taken to task James Petras on this matter, as has Norman Finkelstein, and you can read the arguments in the book, which I found saddening but probably necessary. The reader will have to decide the matter for him/herself. Also earmarked for criticism is Tam Dalyell for his implication of blame for the Iraq war on a 'Jewish' or 'Zionist' 'cabal', a statement which he subsequently retracted in that form.

Marqusee's book is an important contribution to the debate both within and outside the Jewish community. It is also valuable for those in the anti-war movement who need to contest vigorously any attempt to slur the movement as anti-Jewish. The media and political opponents, given half a chance, will paint the movement with an anti-Semitic brush. It is therefore in this context that we must remember that support for Zionism and the actions of the Israeli state are only supported by the West because the state of Israel in its present form corresponds to their interests, as a useful component for keeping the lid on attempts by any of the Middle Eastern nations to pursue policies conflicting with Western interests. It is, perhaps, also that the Israeli state has another useful purpose, as Marquees mentions: it was Winston Churchill who seemingly saw Zionism as the cure for the Jewish disease, Bolshevism.

John Daniels

Bin Laden in Bosnia

John R. Schindler, ***Unholy Terror: Bosnia, Al Qaeda, and the Rise of Global Jihad,*** **Zenith Press, 388 pages, hardback ISBN 9780760330036, £18.99**

John Schindler is professor of strategy at the United States Naval War College and was for many years the chief Balkan expert with the United States National Security Agency. In this book he has spilt the beans from what he learnt in the Balkan wars of the 1990s and most particularly in the Bosnian war from 1992 to 1995. He assures his readers that he has not revealed any secret documents, but the 35 pages of notes and references in the book show the most extensive research drawing upon the author's mastery of several languages, both European and Arabic. The book will be an eye-opener for those who have gone along with the standard explanation for the Yugoslav tragedy: that it was caused by the so-called 'ethnic cleansing' policy of the Serbs, and of Slobodan Milosevic in particular, with the poor Moslems of Bosnia cast as the chief victims (see in the United State, particularly, Marlise Simons, David Rieff and his mother Susan Sontag, and in Britain Ed Vulliamy, Michael Ignatieff and Alan Little.[1]

There has always been an alternative view to the one demonising the Serbs, a view which I have taken in reporting on the trial of Milosevic before the International Criminal Tribunal for the former Yugoslavia (ICTY) at the Hague (See M. Barratt Brown et al., *The Trial of Slobodan Milosevic 2004*)[2], a view which was strongly urged by Edward Herman and David Peterson from the US (ibid.), who list 23 journalists whose views, they say, were generally ignored. These included Balkan experts such as Diana Johnstone[3] and John Laughland[4].

Alice Mahon, the one-time Labour MP, and member of the Nato Parliamentary Assembly and chair of its Civilian Affairs Committee, for which she made many visits to war-torn Yugoslavia, also holds an alternative view. She appeared as a witness in the last days of the Tribunal's hearings on Milosevic, and added to her support for this contrary view her conviction that the infamous so-called 'Racak massacre', which served as the trigger for the Nato bombing of Belgrade, was primarily an invention of US Ambassador Walker (see M. Barratt Brown, *Slobodan Milosevic and how the US used Al Qaeda in the Balkans, 2006*).[5] On this view, Milosevic and the Serbs were not exonerated of all responsibility for the Yugoslav wars but had to share it with the leaders of the Croats, the Bosnian Muslims and the Kosovan Albanians. The break-up of Yugoslavia, moreover, was then attributed less to internal divisions than to external influence – of the Germans on Slovenia and Croatia, and of the United States on the Bosnian Muslims (see M.Barratt Brown, *From Tito to Milosevic: Yugoslavia the Lost Country, 2005*).[6]

It was particularly the influence of the United States with the Bosnian Moslems that appeared to have led the Bosnian Moslem leader, Alija Izetbegovic, to renege on a UN peace plan that had been negotiated at Lisbon in March of 1992 (see Barratt Brown, 2004). The enthusiasm of Izetbegovic to establish a religious fundamentalist Moslem state in Bosnia was evident to many observers in Bosnia and to some outside. Indeed, Izetbegovic was jailed in 1983 along with others, many from the Muslim Brotherhood in Cairo, for his contacts with Tehran after the Islamic revolution of 1979 in Iran, and for the secret circulation of his book *The Islamic Declaration*. In the post-Tito disintegration of Yugoslavia, he came out of jail in 1988 and founded the Party of Democratic Action (HDA) in Bosnia, with many of the more fundamentalist Moslems, but presented himself, when he became President of Bosnia-Herzegovina, as a moderate to the majority of secular Moslems in Bosnia and likewise to the Western world in general. His presentation was accepted by outside opinion, despite the well known appeal by Izetbegovic for Iranian funding and arms for the Bosnian Moslem army (Barratt Brown, 2005). It had also been revealed at the Tribunal that two journalists – one, Eve-Ann Prentice from the London *Times*, and another, Renate Flottau from *Der Spiegel* in Germany – called as witnesses at Milosevic's trial, claimed to have seen

Osama Bin Laden entering Izetbegovic's office in Sarajevo in 1994, and that Bin Laden himself and the foreign members of the Bosnian army had been issued with Bosnian passports (Barratt Brown, 2006).

All these reports were hotly denied by the Bosnian authorities, and an element of doubt hung over their accuracy. Such doubts can now be dismissed as a result of what is revealed in Schindler's book. This comprises absolutely firm evidence for Izetbegovic's determination, however much he denied it, to build a pure Moslem religious state in Bosnia, for President Clinton's close involvement in supporting Izetbegovic, and, more importantly, in bringing Mujahideen fighters from Afghanistan to Bosnia, for the presence of Osama Bin Laden in Sarajevo, for the Bosnian passport granted to Bin Laden and to many of the 2,000 Mujahideen who fought in the Bosnian Moslem army. To all this confirmation of what many of us suspected, Schindler adds new and unsuspected evidence of the continuing role of Al Qaeda in using Bosnia as the training ground for those who launched the assaults on Khartoum, New York, London, Madrid and Bali (Schindler, pp.296-7). It is an extraordinary indictment.

Two questions remain unanswered: first, why most Western journalists accepted Izetbegovic's pretences and actual lies and supported the Moslems against the Serbs in Bosnia; and, second, why Clinton, apparently against the advice of both the CIA and the War Department, encouraged the Mujahideen to enter Bosnia, to support the Moslem forces. The answer to the first question about journalists, particularly from the United Kingdom, whose bias has to be explained, must be the charisma of Izetbegovic and his extraordinary capacity for concealing his true aims and presenting himself and the Bosnian Moslems as innocent victims of Serbian aggression. Some basic anti-Serb feeling, because of Serb association with Russian Communism, stirred up by German historic Slavo-phobia, may have played a part. But the fact was that the Bosnian Moslems and the Croats, who became allied with them on US instigation, were brilliantly advised by the US public relations company Ruder Finn. (Schindler, p.107). On top of all this, we need to notice the fact that foreign journalists were housed in the Holiday Inn hotel in Sarajevo, which was regularly shelled by Serb forces, and occasionally even from Moslem fire designed to appear to be from Serb guns, to build up anti-Serb feeling (Schindler pp.84 ff. and *passim* in the chapter entitled 'The Great Deceit').

The most extreme example of Izetbegovic's deception is the true story of the Srebrenica massacre, which has entered the history books as the cold-blooded murder by the Serbs of seven, eight or even more thousand Moslems – men, women and children – rounded up in Srebrenica. Schindler accepts the account provided by Generals Morillon and Lewis MacKenzie, commanders of the UN forces in Bosnia, and by the Dutch peace keeping force, viz. that Izetbegovic deliberately withdrew the Muslim forces so that the Serbs were able to enter Srebrenica unopposed and to carry out the killings of Muslim men in revenge for the thousands of Serbs killed over the previous years in the villages around Srebrenica by Moslem forces under the command of Naser Oric. Some 1,300 bodies of Moslem dead men have been exhumed in Srebrenica, some of them with their hands tied behind their backs for execution. In all conscience this is a terrible number, but it is not seven or eight thousand. Several thousand women and children were reported by the Red Cross to have escaped to Sarajevo and Tuzla. The reason for Izetbegovic's action, as he claimed himself, was that Clinton had said that the US forces could not intervene with air strikes against the Serb base at Pale unless there was a major massacre of Muslims by the Serbs to provide the excuse (Schindler, pp.317-8).

This brings us to the decisions of President Clinton. What led him, despite lacking support from either his Intelligence Services or the Defence Department, to give every kind of allowance to Izetbegovic, including the clandestine supply of arms, in contravention of UN resolutions, even to the extent of encouraging Mujahideen to join the Bosnian army? The US had supported Mujahideen recruits from Saudi Arabia and other Arab countries, including Osama Bin Laden, to help to defeat the Russians in Afghanistan, but why bring them out to Bosnia? US ambassador Richard Holbrooke was to argue that the Mujahideen provided a useful counter in Bosnia to the influence over Izetbegovic of Iran, but Holbrooke had himself earlier advocated the recruiting of forces from Arab countries (Schindler, pp. 181 and 273-4). Clinton was said to have argued that support for some Muslim forces would show that he had other friends in the Near East besides the Jews. He also said in a remarkable distortion of history that the Serbs had started two world wars and he wasn't going to see them start a third (Schindller p 110).

One reason for Clinton's enthusiasm for the Bosnian Muslims is suggested by Schindler (Schindler p.110). This was Clinton's desire to challenge European interests in the Balkans, particularly those of Germany in Slovenia and Croatia. But there can be no doubt that the main influence on Clinton came from the State Department under Mrs Albright. Their preoccupation was to find a new role for Nato after the collapse of the Soviet Union. This new role was encapsulated in the idea of 'humanitarian intervention', which was to replace the previous understanding of the UN that there should be no intervention in the affairs of any state unless its government had committed aggression against another state. The first war against Saddam Hussein fulfilled that criterion, but the second did not. Nor did the bombing of Belgrade; and it is those among liberal opinion in the US and from the left in the United Kingdom and elsewhere in Europe, who supported that bombing, who are the most anxious that the demonisation of the Serbs and of Milosevic should stick. When Clinton was thinking about the problem, he simply went along with the passionate cries for the defence of the poor Muslims in Bosnia (Schindler pp.90-1).

What Clinton could not *perhaps* have known, though his intelligence service should have warned him, was that Bosnia would be used as a training ground for Muslim extremists, including Mujahideen from Afghanistan, but many also from Saudi Arabia, Algeria, Pakistan, the Muslim Brotherhood in Egypt, who would together be responsible for the acts of terror in Khartoum, East Africa, New York, Washington, London, Madrid and Bali. Schindler gives the names and biographies of these men; and this detailed denouncement, which he is able to make from his own knowledge, makes the most telling revelation in the book. (Schindler, pp. 295 ff. in the section headed 'Bosnia and Bin Laden: the continuing threat'). The particular tragedy to which Schindler refers is the conversion of the Bosnian Muslims to the extreme forms of Muslim sharia law, such as forcing women to wear the veil on pain of torture and even execution (Schindler, p.321).

A most peculiar twist to Schindler's story is that he can find no evidence of intervention against the Mujahideen by the large UN force (UNPROFOR) stationed in Bosnia after the war was over. No attempt was made to close down the camps where Mujahideen and other Muslim recruits were being trained for terrorist activity. After the year 2002, Paddy (Lord) Ashdown served as the UN High Representative in Sarajevo and seems either not to have known what was going on or to have turned a blind eye to what he saw. More than that, Ashdown not only favoured the more fundamentalist Muslims, but actually fired in 2002 the one member of the Bosnian Government, Munir Alibabic, who was seriously trying to control the Mujahideen and tackle the corruption associated with their activities (Schindler, pp.290ff).

The question remains: why the surprising blindness? The answer must again be the general demonisation of the Serbs, and most particularly of Milosevic, and the need to offer some justification for the illegal and devastatingly destructive bombing of Belgrade by Nato forces as an act of so-called 'humanitarian intervention' in the civil war in Kosovo. In this war the Serbs were cast as the aggressors and the Muslim Albanians with their Mujahideen mercenaries from Bosnia as the victims. Ashdown had been in Kosovo, and, as he explained to the Tribunal in the Milosevic case, he blamed the Serbs for what happened there. He does not mention the presence of Mujahideen in Kosovo, which is not surprising as they were all passing as Bosnians with Bosnian passports. He does comment on the drug running that he had seen among the Albanians (Barratt Brown, 2004). But his silence over the terrorist training camps in Bosnia, whose presence was referred to, in 2004, in the *Washington Post*, *Le Figaro*, and several Spanish papers,(Schindler, pp. 297-8) remains hard to explain.

Bosnian veterans are shown by Schindler to have been involved in terrorist actions in 2005, and the Bosnian connection was duly reported in the *Washington Post* and the *Sunday Times* in December 2005 (Schindler, pp. 318-319). Finally, Schindler refers to his own article on the Bosnian-based jihad 'Defeating the Sixth Column: Intelligence and Strategy in the War on Islamist Terrorism', published in *Orbis*, Fall, 2005 (Schindler, p.323).

The last sentence of the book under review here, published two years later, in 2007, concludes Schindler's analysis. It reads ominously:

'If Bosnia, the most pro-Western society in the *umma,* can be converted into a Jihardistan through domestic deceit, violent conflict and misguided international intervention, nowhere in the Muslim world can be judged safe from dangerous radicalisation. The lesson of Bosnia is that it happened.' (Schindler, p, 325)

Michael Barratt Brown

References

1. David Rieff, *Slaughterhouse: Bosnia and the Failure of the West*, Simon & Schuster, New York, 1995
   Marlise Simons, *New York Times*, 1998-2003, quoted passim by Edward S. Herman & David Peterson, in *The Trial of Slobodan Milosevic*, Spokesman, 2004
   Ed Vulliamy, *Seasons in Hell, Understanding Bosnia's War*, St. Martins New York,1994
   Michael Ignatieff, *The Warrior's Honour: Ethnic War and the Modern Conscience*, Chatto & Windus, 1998
   Alan Little, e.g. in the *Guardian*, 06.01.03
2. Michael Barratt Brown, *The Trial of Slobodan Milosevic*, Spokesman, 2004
3. Diana Johnstone, *Fools' Crusade*, Pluto Press, 2002
4. John Laughland, *Travesty: The Trial of Slobodan Milosevic*, Pluto Press, 2007
5. Michael Barratt Brown, 'Slobodan Milosevic and how the US used Al Qaeda in the Balkans', *Debatte: Journal of Contemporary Central and Eastern Europe*, August 2006, pp. 161-165
6. Michael Barratt Brown, *From Tito to Milosevic: Yugoslavia, the Lost Country*, Merlin Press, 2005

Retrenchment

Francis G. Castles (editor), *The Disappearing State?*, Edward Elgar Publishing, 296 pages, hardback ISBN 9781845422974, £69.95, paperback ISBN 9781847209863, £25

This collection of statistical essays examines the behaviour of public expenditure in Organisation for Economic Co-operation and Development countries since the neoliberal revolution in economic policy in the 1970s and 1980s. It is based on the papers discussed at a workshop of researchers in this field in 2006, and is very much one for technical experts, rather than the more general reader, economist or not. It does contain, however, a variety of statistics of different forms of government expenditure which could be of wider interest.

The expenditure statistics are all expressed in terms of percentages of gross domestic product (gdp) – but without any discussion of the implications of this measure. Changes in this ratio are regarded as 'increases' or 'decreases' in public expenditure. The significance of this approach merits careful consideration. At first sight, maintenance of expenditure on say, health or education, as a constant proportion of gdp might be regarded as implying a growth in resources for this purpose in line with the growth in the economy as a whole. But this is not the case, because in these fields there is little or no scope for increases in productivity as there is elsewhere in the economy. Fewer nurses per 100 patients, or teachers per 100 students, mean a decline in standards, not an increase in productivity; and if nurses' and teachers' pay goes up in line with average pay across the economy as a whole, merely keeping the number of nurses or teachers as a constant proportion of the total working population means that expenditure in these fields will remain a constant proportion of gdp. The same applies to most other fields of public expenditure, particularly on the military. So the use of expenditure to gdp ratios as a yardstick is a reasonable one, as long as its implications are understood.

The authors divide expenditure into 'social' and 'core'. Social expenditure covers transfer payments, for example, pensions, health and other caring functions. Core expenditure is the residual and includes defence, education and debt interest. Surprisingly perhaps, social spending continued to grow in the 1980s and 1990s, but core expenditure fell – a major factor here being reductions in defence spending with the end of the Cold War. Between 1980 and 2001, average OECD levels of social spending rose from 18.8 per cent in 1980 to 22.7 per cent in 2001; whereas the average for core spending fell from 24.3 per cent to 20.8 per cent. For a smaller group of 10 countries with significant military expenditure, defence spending fell from 3.0 per cent of gdp in 1980 to 1.9 per cent in 2000. This reflected a reduction in Russian defence expenditure of over 75 per cent at the end of the 1980s.

The cost of state overhead expenditure needed to keep governments running is difficult to disentangle. But with increasing pressure for devolution within the nation state on the one hand, and greater cooperation between states on the other, it is interesting to note that the number of governing units can significantly affect total expenditure. France, despite its reputation for centralisation, has nearly 37,000 units of government, from the local communes up. The United Kingdom, by contrast, has less than 500. This partly explains the fact that expenditure on state overheads in France was 3.8 per cent of gdp in 2002, as against 2.2 per cent in the UK.

The key point that does not emerge from the essays is that as countries become more prosperous it would be natural for them to devote more of their resources to education and health – whether they are publicly or privately funded: the way they are financed can well reflect a left/right political divide. If state education or the NHS fail to deliver acceptable standards of service, more people will be prepared to send their children to private schools or take out private health insurance; and the Tories may devise financial incentives to make it easier for them to do so.

It is worrying that New Labour seem to be impervious to the need to divert more resources to improve standards in these fields. This year's Budget estimated that current expenditure would, if anything, decline rather than increase as a share of gdp, falling from its current level of 38.4 per cent to 37.5 per cent in 2012-13. This is not compatible with meeting the electorate's aspirations for better public services. Labour ministers need to recognise the unpalatable fact that meeting these aspirations will inevitably involve higher taxation, and ensure that this is levied in a progressive manner. This means relying on raising Income Tax on higher incomes, and Inheritance Tax on larger estates and avoiding further increases on sales taxes, which fall most heavily on lower income groups. It is unrealistic to discuss future levels of public expenditure without considering the tax changes needed to support them.

John Grieve Smith

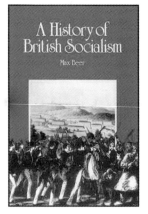